Workbook for Kaplan and Saccuzzo's

PSYCHOLOGICAL TESTING
Principles, Applications, and Issues

FOURTH EDITION

Carma A. Heitzmann
Department of Veteran Affairs
Palo Alto Health Care System

Brooks/Cole Publishing Company

I(T)P® An International Thomson Publishing Company

Pacific Grove • Albany • Belmont • Bonn • Boston • Cincinnati
Detroit • Johannesburg • London • Madrid • Melbourne • Mexico City
New York • Paris • Singapore • Tokyo • Toronto • Washington

Assistant Editor: *Faith B. Stoddard*
Cover Design & Illustration: *Cloyce Wall*
Editorial Assistant: *Nancy Conti*
Marketing Team: *Gay Meixel and Romy Taormina*
Production Editor: *Mary Vezilich*
Printing and Binding: *Malloy Lithographing, Inc.*

For more information, contact:

BROOKS/COLE PUBLISHING COMPANY
511 Forest Lodge Road
Pacific Grove, CA 93950
USA

International Thomson Publishing Europe
Berkshire House 168-173
High Holborn
London WC1V 7AA
England

Thomas Nelson Australia
102 Dodds Street
South Melbourne, 3205
Victoria, Australia

Nelson Canada
1120 Birchmount Road
Scarborough, Ontario
Canada M1K 5G4

International Thomson Editores
Seneca 53
Col. Polanco
México, D. F., México, C. P. 11560

International Thomson Publishing Japan
Hirakawacho Kyowa Building, 3F
2-2-1 Hirakawacho
Chiyoda-ku, Tokyo 102
Japan

International Thomson Publishing Asia
221 Henderson Road
#05-10 Henderson Building
Singapore 0315

International Thomson Publishing GmbH
Königswinterer Strasse 418
53227 Bonn
Germany

Printed in the United States of America

5   4   3   2   1

ISBN 0-534-34375-9

Preface

The *Student's Workbook* to accompany *Psychological Testing: Principles, Applications, and Issues* (4th ed.), was designed to assist the student in understanding and applying the issues presented in the textbook. It should also be useful in assisting students to prepare for examinations. The workbook is meant to supplement the textbook material and each chapter should be completed following a careful reading of the corresponding text. Each workbook chapter is divided into a number of sections.

The first section in each chapter asks the reader to identify important terms, concepts, and names. It is recommended that the student attempt to complete this section before continuing through the workbook chapter, since it provides the foundation for the remainder of the exercises. These items are presented again at the end of the chapter along with the page numbers on which they can be located in the textbook.

Second, fill-in questions are presented. Answers and corresponding page numbers for further reference are found at the end of the chapter.

Third, a number of multiple-choice questions are provided. Again, the answers and corresponding textbook page numbers are listed in the answer section. These and the fill-in questions are intended not only to assist the student in understanding the issues involved in psychological testing, but also to illustrate the types of questions one may encounter on an examination.

Computational problems compromise the fourth feature of the workbook. These are found only in those chapters referring to statistical methods. In the answer section these problems have been worked out in an easy to follow, step-by-step fashion. Whether or not your instructor requires you to calculate similar problems on exams, these exercises will help to familiarize you with some of the applied aspects of statistics in psychology.

Finally, thought questions are presented. In most cases these questions ask you to apply the information found in the textbook to a novel situation or to go somewhat beyond the material that is presented. When appropriate, the relevant textbook page numbers are provided. The primary purposes of this section are to stimulate thought and discussion and to challenge the student to think about psychological testing and measurement in a more global context.

Contents

Chapter 1 Introduction   1

Chapter 2 Norms and Basic Statistics for Testing   9

Chapter 3 Correlation and Regression   21

Chapter 4 Reliability   32

Chapter 5 Validity   37

Chapter 6 Building a Test   42

Chapter 7 Selection and Decision Analysis   47

Chapter 8 Test Administration   52

Chapter 9 Interview Techniques   56

Chapter 10 Tests of Mental Ability: The Binet Scale   61

Chapter 11 The Wechsler Intelligence Scales   66

Chapter 12 Other Individual Tests of Ability   71

Chapter 13 Group Ability Tests: Intelligence
           Achievement and Aptitude   77

Chapter 14 Tests for Choosing Careers   83

Chapter 15 Structured Personality Tests   90

Chapter 16 Projective Personality Tests   98

Chapter 17 Alternatives to Traditional
           Psychological Tests   103

Chapter 18 Measures of Anxiety and Stress   109

Chapter 19 Testing in Health Care Settings   113

Chapter 20 Test Bias   119

Chapter 21 Testing and the Law   125

Chapter 22 The Future of Psychological Testing   131

Chapter 1

Introduction

Terms, Concepts, and Names

Briefly identify the following:

test_____
_____

psychological test_____
_____

overt behavior_____
_____

covert behavior_____
_____

individual test_____
_____

group test_____
_____

ability test_____
_____

achievement_____
_____

aptitude_____
_____

intelligence_____
_____

human ability_____
_____

personality test_____
_____

structured personality test_____
_____

projective personality test_____
_____
_____

psychological testing_____
_____

principles of psychological testing_____
_____

reliability_____
_____

validity_____
_____

Charles Darwin_____
_____

Sir Frances Galton_____
_____

James McKeen Cattell_____
_____

Wilhelm Wundt_____
_____

Alfred Binet_____
_____

Binet-Simon Scale_____
_____

standardization sample_____
_____

representative sample_____
_____

mental age_____
_____

L. M. Terman_____
_____

Robert Yerkes_____
_____

Army Alpha_____
_____

Army Beta_____
_____

Wechsler-Bellvue Intelligence Scale_____

trait_____

Woodworth Personal Data Sheet_____

Rorschach_____

David Levy_____

Sam Beck_____

Henry Murray_____

Christina Morgan_____

Thematic Apperception Test(TAT)_____

Minnesota Multiphasic Personality Inventory(MMPI)_____

California Psychological Inventory(CPI)_____

factor analysis_____

Sixteen Personality Factor(16PF)_____

Shakow report_____

Fill-in Questions

1. A(n) _____ behavior is one that takes place within an individual and cannot be observed. On the other hand, _____ behaviors are observable.
2. _____ refers to the potential for learning a specific skill.
3. Two types of personality tests are _____

and _____.
4. The type of personality test that requires an individual to choose between two or more alternative responses is a(n) _____.
5. The western world most likely learned about testing programs through exposure to the _____.
6. The most basic concept underlying psychological testing is that of _____.
7. The first systematic attempt to evaluate individual differences in human intelligence was by _____.
8. A major difference between the Stanford-Binet and Wechsler-Bellvue Intelligence tests is that _____ _____.
9. One of the goals of traditional personality testing is to measure _____.
10. The test stimulus for structured personality tests tends to be _____, while projective tests provide a(n) _____ stimulus.
11. Factor analytic techniques were employed in the development of the _____.
12. During the 1940s and early 1950s _____ was the major function of clinical psychologists.

Multiple-Choice Questions

1. The use of test batteries was common by the time of the
   a) Ling Dynasty
   b) Han Dynasty
   c) Ming Dynasty
   d) Tam Dynasty
   e) Nam Dynasty

2. The term "mental test" was coined by
   a) James McKeen Cattell
   b) Charles Darwin
   c) Sir Frances Galton
   d) Alfred Binet
   e) Robert Yerkes

3. Who headed the team of psychologists that developed the Army Alpha and Army Beta?
   a) James McKeen Cattell
   b) Alfred Binet
   c) L. M. Terman
   d) Robert Yerkes
   e) J. F. Herbart

4. Which of the following is a group test of human ability for adults that does not require the subject to be literate?

a) Army Alpha
b) Seguin Form Board
c) Stanford-Binet
d) Army Beta
e) Wechsler-Bellvue Intelligence Scale

5. The first structured personality test was the
    a) MMPI
    b) Rorschach
    c) Woodworth Personal Data Sheet
    d) TAT
    e) 16PF

6. The Rorschach was introduced into the United States by
    a) Sam Beck
    b) Herman Rorschach
    c) Christina Morgan
    d) Henry Murray
    e) David Levy

7. Which of the following personality tests is purported
to measure human needs?
    a) Rorschach
    b) MMPI
    c) TAT
    d) CPI
    e) 16PF

Thought Questions

1. Explain the purpose of a standardization sample and
   discuss the characteristics such a sample should
   possess. How might you go about obtaining such a
   sample? (page 17)

_____
_____
_____
_____
_____
_____
_____
_____
_____
_____
_____
_____
_____
_____

2. In what settings are psychological tests most likely to
   be found today? What role does psychological testing
   play in contemporary society and how has this role
   changed since the inception of testing? (pages 12-27)

_____
_____
_____
_____
_____
_____
_____
_____
_____
_____
_____
_____
_____
_____
_____
_____
_____
_____
_____
_____

Answers

Terms, Concepts, and Names

      test (p.7)
      psychological test (p.8)
      overt behavior (p.8)
      covert behavior (p.8)
      individual test (p.9)
      group test (p.9)
      ability test (p.9)
      achievement (p.9)
      aptitude (p.9)
      intelligence (p.10)
      human ability (p.10)
      personality test (p.10)
      structured personality test (p.10)
      projective personality test (p.10)

psychological testing (p.11)
principles of psychological testing (p.11)
reliability (p.12)
validity (p.12)
Charles Darwin (p.14)
Sir Frances Galton (p.14)
James McKeen Cattell (p.14)
Wilhelm Wundt (p.16)
Alfred Binet (p.16)
Binet-Simon Scale (p.16)
standardization sample (p.17)
representative sample (p.17)
mental age (p.17)
L. M. Terman (p.18)
Robert Yerkes (p.18)
Army Alpha (p.18)
Army Beta (p.18)
Wechsler-Bellvue Intelligence Scale (p.19)
trait (p.20)
Woodworth Personal Data Sheet (p.20)
Rorschach (p.21)
David Levy (p.21)
Sam Beck (p.21)
Henry Murray (p.22)
Christina Morgan (p.22)
TAT (p.22)
MMPI (p.22)
CPI (p.23)
factor analysis (p.23)
16PF (p.23)
Shakow report (p.24)

Fill-in Questions

1. covert, overt (p.8)
2. Aptitude (p.9)
3. structured personality tests, projective personality tests (p.10)
4. structured personality test (p.10)
5. Chinese (p.13)
6. individual differences (p.14)
7. Binet (p.16)
8. the Wechsler-Bellvue yields several scores including a performance scale (p.19)
9. traits (p.20)
10. unambiguous, ambiguous (p.21)
11. 16PF (p.23)
12. psychological testing (p.24)

Multiple-Choice Questions

1. b (p.13)
2. a (p.14)
3. d (p.18)
4. d (p.18)
5. c (p.20)
6. e (p.21)
7. c (p.22)

Chapter 2

Norms and Basic Statistics for Testing

Terms, Concepts and Names

Briefly identify the following:

descriptive statistics_____

_____

inferential statistics_____

_____

sample_____

_____

magnitude_____

_____

equal intervals_____

_____

absolute zero_____

_____

nominal scale_____

_____

ordinal scale_____

_____

interval scale_____

_____

ratio scale_____

_____

frequency distribution_____

_____

class interval_____

_____

percentile rank_____

_____

percentiles_____

_____

mean_____
_____

standard devation_____
_____

variance_____
_____

z score_____
_____

standard normal distribution_____
_____

symmetrical binomial probability distribution_____
_____

McCall's T_____
_____

quartile_____
_____

decile_____
_____

stanine_____
_____

age-related norms_____
_____

tracking_____
_____

norm referenced test_____
_____

criterion referenced test_____
_____
_____

Fill-in Questions

1. The purpose of a _____ scale is to name objects.

2. _____ scales have the properties of magnitude and equal intervals, while _____ scales have the properties of magnitude, equal intervals, and absolute

10

zero.

3. The variance of a set of scores is the mean of the
   _____ and is calculated by
   _____, _____, and _____.

4. The standard deviation is the _____ of the
   variance and is represented by _____ when it refers to
   a population and _____ when it refers to a sample.

5. If a score is equal to the mean its z score will be
   _____. If the score is greater than the mean the z
   score will be _____ and if it is less than the
   mean the z score will be _____

6. _____ scores are standard scores with a mean of
   50 and a standard deviation of 10.

Multiple-Choice Questions

1. A scale which allows us to rank individuals or objects
   but not to say anything about the meaning of the
   differences between the ranks is a(n)
      a) nominal scale
      b) interval scale
      c) ordinal scale
      d) ratio scale
      e) magnitude scale

2. In a symmetrical binomial probability distribution, the
   greatest frequency of scores is near the
      a) ends of the distribution
      b) center of the distribution
      c) top of the distribution
      d) bottom of the distribution
      e) cannot say without knowing the range of scores

3. Approximately what percentage of scores fall below the
   mean in a standard normal distribution?
      a) 50%
      b) 34%
      c) 1%
      d) 84%
      e) 16%

4. At approximately what percentile would a score be that
   is two standard deviations below the mean in a standard
   normal distribution?
      a) 16th
      b) 5th
      c) 34th
      d) 2nd
      e) 50th

5. Within the quartile system the third quartile is what percentile?
   a) 50th
   b) 25th
   c) 30th
   d) 75th
   e) 60th

6. What system is standardized to have a mean of 5 and a standard deviation of approximately 2?
   a) decile
   b) McCall's T
   c) stanine
   d) quartile
   e) z score

Computational Problems

1. Determine what your percentile rank would be if you received the tenth highest grade on your psychology exam in a class of 50 students.

2. Find the mean for each of the following sets of numbers.
   a) 6,4,2,9

mean=_____

   b) 5,8,10,3

mean=_____

     c) 14,0,5,8,6

mean=_____

3. For each of the following sets of numbers calculate the
   standard deviation using both the deviation and raw
   score methods found on pages 44-45 of your text. (Note:
   Use the formula for samples.)

     a) 8
       5
       3
       4
       7
       5

deviation_____

raw score_____

     b) 12
       15
       20

8
5

deviation_____

raw score_____

4. Find the z score equivalents for the following scores
   using the formula on page 45 of your text.
     a) 10   z score_____
     b) 5   z score_____
     c) 3   z score_____
     d) 6   z score_____

5. Calculate the raw score equivalents of the following z
   scores given a mean of 10 and a standard deviation of
   2.

a)-2.0

raw score_____

b).5

raw score_____

c)1.5

raw score_____

<u>Thought Questions</u>

1. What purposes do statistical methods serve in our quest
   for scientific understanding?   (page 30)

_____
_____
_____
_____
_____
_____
_____

2. Develop an example of each type of scale; nominal,
   ordinal, interval and ratio.   (pages 32-33)

_____
_____
_____
_____
_____
_____
_____

3. What is the difference between a norm-referenced test
   and a criterion-referenced test? Give a unique example
   of each.

_____

_____
_____
_____
_____
_____
_____
_____
_____
_____

4. Describe the advantages and disadvantages of within
    group norming. (p.57)

_____
_____
_____
_____
_____
_____
_____
_____
_____
_____
_____

<u>Answers</u>

<u>Terms, Concepts, and Names</u>

descriptive statistics (p.30)
inferential statistics (p.30)
sample (p.30)
magnitude (p.30)
equal intervals (p.31)
absolute zero (p.32)
nominal scale (p.32)
ordinal scale (p.32)
interval scale (p.33)
ratio scale (p.33)
frequency distribution (p.34)
class interval (p.35)
percentile rank (p.36)
percentiles (p.41)
mean (p.42)
standard deviation (p.43)
variance (p.43)
z score (p.45)
standard normal distribution (p.47)
symmetrical binomial probability distribution (p.49)
McCall's T (p.53)
quartile (p.54)
decile (p.55)

16

stanine (p.55)
age-related norms (p.56)
tracking (p.59)
norm referenced test (p.62)
criterion referenced test (p.62)

Fill-in Questions

1. nominal (p.32)
2. interval, ratio (p.33)
3. squared deviations around the mean, squaring each deviation, summing them, dividing by N (p.43)
4. square root,   , S (p.43-44)
5. 0, positive, negative (p.45)
6. McCall's T (p.53)

Multiple-Choice Questions

1. c (p.32)
2. b (p.49)
3. a (p.50)
4. d (pgs.49-50)
5. d (p.54)
6. c (p.55)

Computational Problems

1. 1. Determine how many people obtained a score below the score of interest. 50-10=40
    2. Determine how many people were in the group. 50
    3. Divide the number of people below the score of interest (Step1) by the number of people in the group (Step 2). 40÷50=.80
    4. Multiply the result of this division (Step 3) by 100...80x100=80
    5. Percentile rank=**80th**   (pgs.37-38)

2. a) 6+4+2+9=21
        21÷4=5.25
        mean=**5.25**
    b) 5+8+10+3=26
        26÷4=6.5
        mean=**6.5**
    c) 14+0+5+8+6=33
        33÷5=6.6
        mean=**6.6**   (p.42)

3. a)
Deviation Method:
1. Find N by counting the number of observations.
    N=6
2. Find N-1. Subtract 1 from Step 1.
    6-1=5

3. Find $\bar{X}$. Add up all of the scores and divide by the number of scores   (Step 1).
    $8+5.........+5=32$
    $32\div6=5.33$
4. Find $X-\bar{X}$. Subtract $\bar{X}$ (Step 3) from each score.
    $8-5.33=2.67$
    $5-5.33=-.33$
    $3-5.33=-2.33$
    $4-5.33=-1.33$
    $7-5.33=1.67$
    $5-5.33=-.33$
5. Find $\Sigma(X-\bar{X})^2$. Square each of the results from Step 4 and add them up.
    $(2.67^2)+(-.33^2)+(-2.33^2)+(-1.33^2)+(1.67^2)+(-.33^2)=$
    $7.13+.11.........+.11=17.33$
6. Find $S=\sqrt{\dfrac{\Sigma(X-\bar{X})^2}{N-1}}$ Divide Step 5 by Step 2 and take the square root.

    $\sqrt{\dfrac{17.33}{5}}=\sqrt{3.47}=1.86$

    $S=1.86$

Raw Score Method:
1. Find N by counting the number of observations.
    $N=6$
2. Find N-1. Subtract 1 from Step 1.
    $6-1=5$
3. Find ΣX^2. Square each score and then add them up.
    $8^2+5^2.........+5^2=$
    $64+25.........+25=188$
4. Find $(\Sigma X)^2$. Add up all of the scores and square the result.
    $8+5.........+5=32$
    $32^2=1,024$
5. Find $\dfrac{(\Sigma X)^2}{N}$. Divide Step 4 by Step 1.
    $1,024\div6=170.67$
6. Find $\Sigma X^2-\dfrac{(\Sigma X)^2}{N}$. Subtract the result of Step 5 from the result of Step 3.
    $188-170.67=17.33$
7. Find $S=\sqrt{\dfrac{\Sigma X^2-\dfrac{(\Sigma X)^2}{N}}{N-1}}$

    Divide the result of Step 6 by the result of Step 2 and take the square root.
    $\sqrt{\dfrac{17.33}{5}}=\sqrt{3.47}=1.86$

    $S=1.86$

b)
Deviation Method:

1. Find N by counting the number of observations.

   N=5

2. Find N-1. Subtract 1 from Step 1.

   5-1=4

3. Find $\overline{X}$. Add up all of the scores and divide by the number (N) of scores (Step 1).

   12+15.........+5=60

   60÷5=12

4. Find X-$\overline{X}$. Subtract $\overline{X}$ (Step 3) from each score.

   12-12=0

   15-12=3

   20-12=8

   8-12=-4

   5-12=-7

5. Find $\Sigma(X-\overline{X})^2$. Square each of the results from Step 4 and add them up.

   $(0^2)+(3^2)+(8^2)+(-4^2)+(-7^2)=$

   0+9+64+16+49=13

6. Find $S=\sqrt{\dfrac{\Sigma(X-\overline{X})^2}{N-1}}$. Divide Step 5 by Step 2 and take the square root.

   $\sqrt{\dfrac{138}{4}} = \sqrt{34.5}=5.87$

   S=5.87

Raw Score Method:

1. Find N. Count the number of observations.

   N=5

2. Find N-1. Subtract 1 from Step 1.

   5-1=4

3. Find ΣX^2. Square each score and then add them up.

   $12^2+15^2+20^2+8^2+5^2=$

   144+225=.........+25=858

4. Find $(\Sigma X)^2$. Add up all of the scores and square the result.

   12+15..........+5=60

   60^2=3,600

5. Find $\dfrac{(\Sigma X)^2}{N}$ Divide Step 4 by Step 1.

   3,600÷5=720

6. Find $\Sigma X^2-\dfrac{(\Sigma X)^2}{N}$ Subtract the result of Step 5 from the result of Step 3.

   858-720=138

7. Find $S=\sqrt{\dfrac{\Sigma X^2-\dfrac{(\Sigma X)^2}{N}}{}}$ Divide the result of Step 6 by the result of Step 2 and take the square root.

   $\sqrt{\dfrac{138}{4}} = \sqrt{34.5} =5.87$

   S=5.87

4.

1. Find N. Count the number of observations.

N=4
2. Find N-1. Subtract 1 from Step 1.
   4-1=3
3. Find $\overline{X}$. Add up all of the scores and divide by the number (N) of scores (Step 1).
   10+5+3+6=24
   24÷4=6
4. Find $X-\overline{X}$. Subtract $\overline{X}$ (Step 3) from each score.
   10-6=4
   5-6=1
   3-6=-3
   6-6=0
5. Find $\Sigma(X-\overline{X})^2$. Square each of the results from step 4 and add them up.
   $(4^2)+(-1^2)+(-3^2)+(0^2)=$
   16+1+9+0=26
6. Find $S=\sqrt{\dfrac{\Sigma(X-\overline{X})^2}{N-1}}$. Divide Step 5 by Step 2 and take the square root.

   $\sqrt{\dfrac{26}{3}} = \sqrt{8.67} = 2.94$

7. Find the z score equivalents using the formula: $z=\dfrac{X-\overline{X}}{S}$;

   a) $Z=\dfrac{10-6}{2.94} = \dfrac{4}{2.94} = 1.36$

   b) $Z=\dfrac{5-6}{2.94} = \dfrac{-1}{2.94} = -.34$

   c) $Z=\dfrac{3-6}{2.94} = \dfrac{-3}{2.94} = -1.02$

   d) $Z=\dfrac{6-6}{2.94} = \dfrac{0}{2.94} = 0$

5.
Using the formula: $Z=\dfrac{X-\overline{X}}{S}$;

   a) $-2.0 = \dfrac{X-10}{2} = 10+(2.0)(-2)=X$ **X=6**

   b) $.5 = \dfrac{X-10}{2} = 10+(.5)(2)=X$ **X=11**

   c) $1.5 = \dfrac{X-10}{2} = 10+(1.5)(2)=X$ **X=13**

Chapter 3

Correlation and Regression

Terms, Concepts, and Names

Briefly identify the following:

scatter diagram_____

_____

correlation coefficient_____

_____

regression line_____

_____

slope_____

_____

intercept_____

_____

residual_____

_____

Pearson Product Moment Correlation Coefficient_____

_____

normative_____

_____

Spearman's rho_____

_____

biserial correlation_____

_____

phi coefficient_____

_____

standard error of estimate_____

_____

coefficient of determination_____

_____

coefficient of alienation_____

_____

_____

shrinkage_____

_____

cross-validation_____

_____

third variable_____

_____

multivariate analysis_____

_____

multiple regression_____

_____

discriminant analysis_____

_____

factor analysis_____

_____

principal components_____

_____

factor loadings_____

_____

_____

Fill-in Questions

1. Each point on a scatter diagram represents _____
   _____.
2. If the line that comes closest to all the points in a
   scatter diagram is straight, the correlation between
   the two variables is _____, however, if the line
   is curved the correlation is _____.
3. If the scores on X do not give us any information about
   the scores on Y this indicates _____.
4. The _____ describes how much change is expected in
   Y each time X increases by one unit.
5. The regression line is the best-fitting straight line
   through a set of points in a scatter diagram. It is
   found by using the principle of _____.
6. In a correlation the scores for both variables are in
   _____ units and the intercept is always _____.
7. The Pearson Product Moment Correlation Coefficient can
   take any value between _____ and _____.
8. Correlation coefficients can be tested for statistical
   significance using the _____.
9. The _____ is a measure of accuracy of

22

prediction in a correlation and is the standard
deviation of the _____.
10. Correlational techniques only allow us to describe the
relationship between two variables wheras, _____
allow us to examine the relationships among many
variables.

Multiple-Choice Questions

1. In the two scatter diagrams shown below the
relationship between the two variables is
    a) stronger in A than in B
    b) equal in A and B
    c) impossible to determine
    d) stronger in B than in A
    e) none of the above

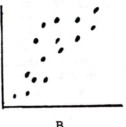

A   B

2. People who drink caffeinated beverages tend to
experience increased alertness and psychomotor
activity. This demonstrates a
    a) positive correlation
    b) negative correlation
    c) zero correlation
    d) not enough information is provided
    e) none of the above

3. Which of the following correlations represents the
strongest relationship between two variables?
    a) .50
    b) .00
    c) -.85
    d) .80
    e) -.10

4. In the formula Y'=a+bx, Y' is the
    a) regression coefficient
    b) raw score of Y
    c) predicted value of Y
    d) intercept
    e) slope

23

5. The point at which the regression line crosses the y axis is the
   a) slope
   b) regression coefficient
   c) predicted value of X
   d) correlation
   e) intercept

6. A method of correlation that is used to find the association between two sets of ranks rather than between continuous variables is
   a) Spearman's rho
   b) point biserial
   c) tetrachoric
   d) phi coefficient
   e) Pearson Product Moment

7. In order to determine the relationship between sex of subject and income level one would use the
   a) phi coefficient
   b) point biserial correlation
   c) Spearman's rho
   d) Pearson Product Moment Correlation Coefficient
   e) any of the above would be suitable

8. The primary purpose of factor analysis is to
   a) determine the relationship between variables
   b) reduce a large set of variables to a smaller composite set
   c) predict some criterion
   d) insure that proper inferences are being made
   e) determine the degree of non-association between variables

Computational Problems

1. An epidemiologist is interested in determining the effect of immunization against chicken pox on the rate of the disease in children. To do so, she sampled six cities across the country and established both the percenatge of children who had been vaccinated and the number of cases of chicken pox per 100 children. Find the correlation coefficient for these two variables using the formula found on page 72 of your text.

	X % of children immunized against chicken pox	Y # of cases of chicken pox per 100 children
A	43	6
B	72	4
C	81	3
D	32	7
E	19	13
F	84	2

Explain the meaning of the resulting correlation
coefficient._____
_____
_____
_____
_____
_____
_____
_____
_____
_____
_____

2.a) Find the correlation coefficient for the following
set of scores.

	X Body Weight	Y number of calories consumed per day (in hundreds)
A	150	20
B	110	18
C	200	30
D	105	12
E	175	21

b) Explain the meaning of the resulting correlation
   coefficient.
_____
_____
_____
_____
_____
_____
_____

c) Plot this relationship on the figure below.

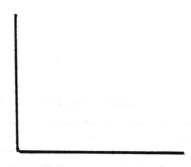

d) What percentage of total variation in the scores on Y
   can be explained by our information about X?

e) Find the coefficient of alienation.

Thought Questions

1. Select a variable of interest and a hypothetical means of predicting it, and plot the relationship on the figure below. In words, explain your diagram.

_____
_____
_____
_____
_____
_____

2. Explain the correlation-causation problem and give an example. (pages 85-86)

_____
_____
_____
_____
_____
_____
_____
_____
_____
_____

3. Discuss possible third variables that may explain the observed relationship between the variables in the second computational problem.

_____
_____
_____
_____
_____
_____
_____
_____

Answers

Terms, Concepts, and Names

scatter diagram (p.66)
correlation coefficient (p.67)

regression line (p.68)
slope (p.70)
intercept (p.70)
residual (p.70)
Pearson Product Moment Correlation Coefficient (p.72)
normative (p.78)
Spearman's rho (p.81)
biserial correlation (p.82)
phi coefficient (p.82)
standard error of estimate (p.84)
coefficient of determination (p.84)
coeffiecient of alienation (p.84)
shrinkage (p.85)
cross-validation (p.85)
third variable (p.85)
multivariate analysis (p.85)
multiple regression (p.87)
discriminant analysis (p.88)
factor analysis (p.89)
principal components (p.92)
factor loadings (p.92)

Fill-in Questions

1. where an individual scored on both X and Y. (p.66)
2. linear, non-linear (p.66-67)
3. no correlation (p.67)
4. slope (p.70)
5. least squares (p.71)
6. z or standard, zero (p.72)
7. -1.0, 1.0 (p.72)
8. t-distribution (p.76)
9. standard error of estimate, residuals (p.84)
10. multivariate analysis (p.85)

Multiple-Choice Questions

1. d
2. a
3. c
4. c (p.70)

5. e (p.70)
6. a (p.82)
7. b (p.83)
8. b (p.92)

Computational Problems

1. Find N by counting the number of paired observations.
   N=6
2. Find ΣX by summing the X scores.
   43+72..........+84=331
3. Find ΣY by summing the Y scores.
   6+4.........+2=35

4. Find ΣX^2. Square each X score and then sum them.
   1849+5184..........+7,056=22,035
5. Find ΣY^2. Square each Y score and then sum them.
   36+16..........+4=283
6. Find ΣXY. For each pair of observations multiply X by Y and then sum the products.
   (43x6)+(72x4)..........+(84x2)=
   258+288..........+168=1,428
7. Find $(\Sigma X)^2$ by squaring the result of Step 2.
   331^2=109,561
8. Find $(\Sigma Y)^2$ by squaring the result of Step 3.
   35^2=1,225
9. Find $N\Sigma XY$ by multiplying the results of Steps 1 and 6.
   6x1,428=8,568
10. Find $(\Sigma X)(\Sigma Y)$ by multiplying the results of Steps 2 and 3.
    331x35=11,585
11. Find $N\Sigma XY-(\Sigma X)(\Sigma Y)$ by subtracting the result of Step 10 from the results of Step 9.
    8,568-11,585=-3,017
12. Find $N\Sigma X^2$ by multiplying the results of Steps 1 and 4.
    6x22,035=132,210
13. Find $N\Sigma X^2-(\Sigma X)^2$ by subtracting the result of Step 7 from Step 12.
    132,210-109,561=22,649
14. Find $N\Sigma Y^2$ by multiplying the results of Steps 1 and 5.
    6x283=1,698
15. Find $N\Sigma Y^2-(\Sigma Y)^2$ by subtracting the result of Step 8 from Step 14.
    1,698-1,225=473
16. Find $\sqrt{[N\Sigma X^2-(\Sigma X)^2][N\Sigma Y^2-(\Sigma Y)^2]}$ by multiplying the results of Steps 13 and 15 and then taking the square root of the product.
    $\sqrt{22,649\times473}$ =$\sqrt{10,712,977}$ =3,273.07
17. Find $r=\dfrac{N\Sigma XY-(\Sigma X)(\Sigma Y)}{\sqrt{[N\Sigma X^2-(\Sigma X)^2][N\Sigma Y^2-(\Sigma Y)^2]}}$
    by dividing the results of Step 11 by Step 16.
    -3,017÷3,273.07=-.92
    r=-.92

2.a)
1. Find N by counting the number of paired observations.
   N=5
2. Find ΣX by summing the X scores.
   150+110+200+105+175=740
3. Find ΣY by summing the Y scores.
   20+18+30+12+21=101
4. Find ΣX^2. Square each X score and then sum them.
   22,500+12,100+40000+11,025+30,625=116,250
5. Find ΣY^2. Square each Y score and then sum them up.
   400+324+900+144+441=2,209

6. Find ΣXY. For each pair of observations multiply X by Y. Then sum the products.
   (150x20)+(110x18)......=
   3,000+1,980+6,000+1,260+3,675=15,915
7. Find $(ΣX)^2$ by squaring the result of Step 2.
   740^2=547,600
8. Find $(ΣY)^2$ by squaring the result of Step 3.
   101^2=10,201
9. Find NΣXY by multiplying the results of Steps 1 and 6.
   5x15,915=79,575
10. Find (ΣX)(ΣY) by multiplying the results of Steps 2 and 3.
   740x101=74,740
11. Find NΣXY-(ΣX)(ΣY) by subtracting the result of Step 10 from the result of Step 9. 79,575-74,740=4,835
12. Find $NΣX^2$ by multiplying the results of Steps 1 and 4.
   5x116,250=581,250
13. Find $NΣX^2-(ΣX)^2$ by subtracting the result of Step 7 from Step 12.
   58,1250-547,600=33,650
14. Find $NΣY^2$ by multiplying the results of Steps 1 and 5.
   5x2,209=11,045
15. Find $NΣY^2-(ΣY)^2$ by subtracting the result of Step 8 from Step 14.
   11,045-10,201=844
16. Find $\sqrt{[NΣX^2-(ΣX)^2][NΣY^2-(ΣY)^2]}$ by multiplying Steps 13 and 15 and then taking the square root of the product.
   $\sqrt{33,650\times844}$= $\sqrt{28,400,600}$= 5,329.22
17. Find $r=\dfrac{NΣXY-(ΣX)(ΣY)}{\sqrt{[NΣX^2-(ΣX)^2][NΣY^2-(ΣY)^2]}}$
   by dividing the results of Step11 by Step16.
   4,835÷5,329.22=.91
   r=.91

b) A positive correlation coefficient of .91 indicates that there is a strong relationship between number of calories consumed per day and body weight. The more calories consumed the greater the weight.

c)
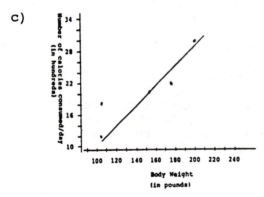

30

d) coefficient of determination= correlation coefficient squared or
$.91^2=.83$ (p.87)

e) coefficient of alienation= the square root of 1-coefficient of determination or $\sqrt{1-.83}=\sqrt{.17}=.41$
(p.87)

Chapter 4

Reliability

Terms, Concepts and Names

Briefly identify the following:

classical test score theory_____

_____

measurement error _____

_____

standard error of measurement_____

_____

test-retest reliability_____

_____

carry-over effect_____

_____

practice effect_____

_____

parallel forms_____

_____

domain sampling_____

_____

split-half method_____

_____

Spearman-Brown formula_____

_____

internal consistency_____

_____

Kuder-Richardson 20_____

_____

covariance_____

_____

coefficient alpha_____

_____

difference score_____
_____
_____

prophecy formula_____
_____

discriminability analysis_____
_____

correction for attenuation_____
_____
_____

Fill-in Questions

1. Theoretically, an observed score is composed of
_____ and _____.
2. Because classical test theory assumes that errors of
measurement are random the distribution of errors
should be _____.
3. The reliability coefficient is the ratio of the
variance of the _____ of a test to the _____.
4. When the same group of people is administered the same
test at two different points in time an assessment of
_____ is being made.
5. The Speraman-Brown formula corrects for
_____.
6. All _____ methods evaluate the extent to
which different test items measure the same ability or
trait.
7. Two approaches to improve the reliability of a test are
to _____ and _____.
8. Attenuations of potential correlations are caused by
_____.

Multiple-Choice Questions

1. If a researcher is attempting to assess the reliability
of a measure of depression the method of choice would
be
   a) internal consistency
   b) time sampling
   c) the test-retest method
   d) both c and d
   e) both a and c

2. The odd-even system is an example of
   a) the split-half method

b) internal consistency
c) time sampling
d) both a and b
e) all of the above

3. The method for estimating the internal consistency of a test that simultaneously considers all of the possible ways of splitting the items is the
   a) the Spearman-Brown formula
   b) the Kuder-Richardson formula
   c) Cronbach's alphas
   d) the odd-even method
   e) the parallel forms method

4. Approximately what value must a reliability coefficient have for most purposes in basic research?
   a) .90
   b) .50
   c) .70
   d) .30
   e) 1.0

5. Under the rubric of the factor analytic approach to test construction, tests will be more reliable if they are
   a) lengthy
   b) multi-dimensional
   c) brief
   d) uni-dimensional
   e) criterion-referenced

Thought Questions

1. Discuss some of the problems facing an investigator who uses a measure with questionable reliability to assess a group of parents before and after a parent effectiveness workshop.

_____
_____
_____
_____
_____
_____
_____
_____
_____
_____
_____
_____

2. Describe some of the advantages and disadvantages associated with behavioral observation techniques and provide an example. (pages 115-118)

_____
_____
_____
_____
_____
_____
_____
_____
_____
_____
_____
_____
_____
_____

Answers

Terms, Names, and Concepts

classical test score theory (p.100)
measurement error (p.100)
standard error of measurement (p.102)
test-retest reliability (p.103)
carry-over effect (p.104)
practice effect (p.104)
parallel forms (p.106)
domain sampling (p.106)
split-half method (p.108)
Spearman-Brown formula (p.109)
internal consistency (p.110)
Kuder-Richardson 20 (p.110)
covariance (p.111)
coefficient alpha (p.112)
difference score (p.113)
prophecy formula (p.122)
discriminability analysis (p.124)
correction for attenuation (p.124)

Fill-in Questions

1. true score, error (p.100)
2. bell-shaped (p.101)

3. true scores, observed score (p.103)
4. test-retest reliability (p.103)
5. deflated reliability due to half-length tests (p.109)
6. internal consistency (p.113)
7. increase the number of items, throw out items that decrease reliability (p.122)
8. measurement error (p.124)

Multiple-Choice Questions

1. a (p.103)
2. d (p.109)
3. b (p.110)
4. c (p.121)
5. d (p.124)

Chapter 5

Validity

Terms, Concepts, and Names

Briefly identify the following:

validity_____

_____

face validity_____

_____

content validity_____

_____

criterion validity_____

_____

predictive validity_____

_____

concurrent validity_____

_____

validity coefficient_____

_____

restricted range_____

_____

generalizability_____

_____

construct validity_____

_____

convergent evidence_____

_____

discriminant evidence_____

_____

_____

Fill-in Questions

1. Although not technically a form of validity _____ implies that the items on a test are reasonably related to the perceived purpose of the test.
2. Two types of criterion related validity are _____ and _____.
3. _____ validity refers to the simultaneous relationship between the test and the criterion.
4. The correlation between a test and the criterion is referred to as a(n) _____.
5. The process of construct validation is necessary when no _____ is available which defines the object of inquiry.
6. To develop a test with construct validity both _____ and _____ evidence are essential.
7. Several measures are already available which are purported to assess anxiety. In order to prove that a new measure of anxiety is needed, the test must measure a _____ aspect of anxiety and, therefore, _____ of validity should be provided.

Multiple-Choice Questions

1. The evidence is logical rather than statistical for
   a) face validity and criterion validity
   b) face validity and predictive validity
   c) criterion validity and content validity
   d) content validity and face validity
   e) content validity and concurrent validity

2. A test which allows us to identify individuals who are likely to become schizophrenic has
   a) face validity
   b) predictive validity
   c) criterion validity
   d) both a and c
   e) both b and c

3. If, for example, a validity coefficient of .50 between a written test of driving ability and actual skills as a driver was found, what percentage of the variation in driving ability would be accounted for as a result of the information from the test?
   a) 10%
   b) 25%
   c) 5%
   d) 50%
   e) 1%

4. A variable with a "restricted range" is problematic
   with regard to the estimation of a validity coefficient
   due to a lack of
   a) criterion validity
   b) variability
   c) adequate sample size
   d) cross validation
   e) representativenes

5. A researcher seeking to develop a measure of depression
   cites a moderate correlation between her measure and
   the Beck Depression Inventory as evidence of the test's
   validity. What type of validity documentation does this
   provide?
   a) convergent validity
   b) predictive validity
   c) discriminant validity
   d) content validity
   e) face validity

Thought Questions

1. Choose a topic of interest and outline the types of
   items you would want to include in an assessment device
   to ensure that your measure has content validity. Also
   discuss other factors that may influence an
   individual's performance on this test. (pgs.132-134)

_____
_____
_____
_____
_____
_____
_____
_____
_____
_____
_____
_____
_____
_____
_____
_____
_____
_____
_____
_____
_____
_____

_____
_____
_____
_____
_____
_____
_____
_____
_____

2. Select three of the eight recommended criteria for evaluation of validity coefficients found on page 138-143 of your text, and develop a unique example of each that would demonstrate that a test may <u>not</u> be valid.

_____
_____
_____
_____
_____
_____
_____
_____
_____
_____
_____
_____
_____
_____
_____
_____
_____
_____
_____
_____
_____
_____
_____
_____

Answers

<u>Terms, Concepts, and Names</u>

      validity (p.131)
      face validity (p.132)
      content validity (p.132)
      criterion validity (p.134)
      predictive validity (p.134)

concurrent validity (p.134)
validity coefficient (p.135)
restricted range (p.142)
generalizability (p.142)
construct validity (p.143)
convergent evidence (p.146)
discriminant evidence (p.148)

Fill-in Questions

1. face validity (p.132)
2. predictive, concurrent (p.134)
3. concurrent (p.134)
4. validity coefficient (p.135)
5. criterion (p.144)
6. discriminant, convergent (p.146)
7. unique, discriminant evidence (p.148)

Multiple-Choice Questions

1. d (p.133)
2. e (p.134)
3. b (p.136)
4. b (p.142)
5. a (p.146)

Chapter 6

Building a Test

Terms, Concepts, and Names

Briefly identify the following:

dichotomous format_____

_____

polytomous format_____

_____

distractors_____

_____

Likert format_____

_____

category format_____

_____

Q-sort_____

_____

item analysis_____

_____

item difficulty_____

_____

discrmination index_____

_____

point biserial correlation_____

_____

item characteristic curve_____

_____

item response theory (IRT)_____

_____

internal criteria_____

_____

criterion-referenced test_____

_____

_____

Fill-in Questions

1. Item reliability on multiple-choice tests is increased when the _____ chosen are likely to be selected as alternative responses.

2. Correction formulas are sometimes employed with tests having a polytomous format in order to _____.

3. One difficulty that has been encountered with the use of _____ formats is that responses tend to be affected by the groupings of the items being rated.

4. The basic methods involved in item analysis are assessment of _____ and _____.

5. An optimum item difficulty level is usually about halfway between _____ and _____.

6. A _____ is a test item that is answered correctly more often by the group of students who have done poorly on the test than by those who have done well.

7. The _____ is the least frequent score in a frequency polygon and is used as a cutting point when evaluating the items in a criterion-referenced test.

Multiple-Choice Questions

1. A test format which is typically used for attitude measurement is the
   a) checklist format
   b) dichotomous format
   c) category format
   d) Likert format
   e) polychotomous format

2. One method for measuring chronic pain asks the respondent to group statements according to how accurately they describe his or her discomfort. This would be an example of the
   a) Q-sort format
   b) checklist format
   c) Likert format
   d) category format
   e) none of the above

3. If 50% of the individuals taking a particular test get a certain item correct the difficulty (or easiness) level of that item would be
   a) .05
   b) .25

c) .50
d) .10
e) 2.5

4. The optimum difficulty level for a five choice multiple-choice item is approximately
   a) .625
   b) .600
   c) .500
   d) .665
   e) .584

5. The extreme group method is one way to determine
   a) item characteristic curves
   b) item discriminability
   c) item difficulty
   d) item reliability
   e) all of the above

6. Which of the following item characteristic curves displays the "best" test item?

a)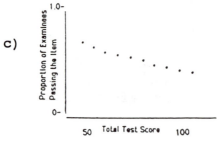

b)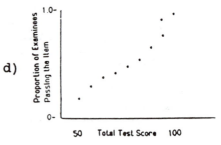

c)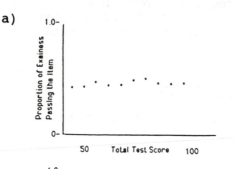

d)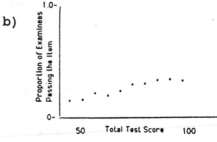

e)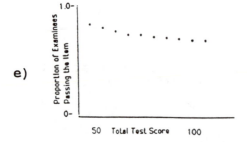

1. Choose one of the item formats discussed on pages 153-159 of your text and describe a test that you might construct using this framework. Also provide your reasons for selecting this format and discuss some of its advantages and disadvantages.

_____
_____
_____
_____
_____
_____
_____
_____
_____
_____
_____
_____
_____
_____
_____
_____
_____
_____

2. Develop several test items and describe methods for analyzing the appropriateness or inappropriateness of their inclusion on a test. (Hint: It may be helpful to actually "administer" these items to a group of friends.) (pgs.160-170)

_____
_____
_____
_____
_____
_____
_____
_____
_____
_____
_____
_____
_____
_____
_____

Answers

<u>Terms, Concepts, and Names</u>

dichotomous format (p.153)
polytomous format (p.153)
distractors (p.154)
Likert format (p.156)
category format (p.156)
Q-sort (p.158)
item analysis (p.160)
item difficulty (p.160)
discrimination index (p.162)
point biserial correlation (p.162)
item characteristic curve (p.164)
item response theory (IRT) (p.167)
internal criteria (p.169)
criterion-referenced test (p.170)

<u>Fill-in Questions</u>

1. distractors (p.154)
2. correct for guessing (pgs.154-155)
3. category (p.157)
4. item difficulty, item discriminability (p.160)
5. 100% of the respondents getting the item correct, the level of success by chance alone (p.161)
6. negative discriminator (p.163)
7. antimode (p.170)

<u>Multiple-Choice Questions</u>

1. d (p.156)
2. a (p.158)
3. c (p.161)
4. b (p.161)
5. b (p.162)
6. d (pgs.165-166)

Chapter 7

Selection and Decision Analysis

Terms, Concepts and Names

Briefly identify the following:

cutting score_____
_____

hit rate_____
_____

base rate_____
_____

false negatives_____
_____

false positives_____
_____

Taylor-Russel tables_____
_____

utility theory_____
_____

incremental validity_____
_____

Tests in Print IV_____
_____

Mental Measurements Yearbook_____
_____
_____

Fill-in Questions

1. The _____ is a short booklet which
   provides a set of standards for test developers and
   users.
2. Among the questions that should be answerd in a test
   manual are those pertaining to practical
   considerations, scoring, _____, _____, and

3. The hit rate of a test is_____.
4. In order for a test to be considered useful, it must
   provide more information than would be known from the
   _____ alone.
5. In terms of the Taylor-Russel tables, a test is most
   useful when the _____ is high and the
   _____ is low.
6. Success as defined by the Taylor-Russel tables requires
   that the criterion be a(n) _____ variable, wheras
   tables based on _____ have attempted to
   define levels of success.
7. Even if a test is reliable and valid it should not be
   used if it does not have _____.

Multiple-Choice Questions

1. On the basis of a psychological test an individual is
   identified as schizophrenic. An interview reveals
   schizophrenic thinking and a past history of
   psychiatric hospitalization. This case best illustrates
   a:
   a) false negative
   b) "miss"
   c) false positive
   d) "hit"
   e) both c and d

2. If a test were available that could identify those
   persons most likely to suffer heart attacks it would be
   more costly and dangerous to have a:
   a) high cutting score
   b) low cutting score
   c) false negative
   d) false positive
   e) both a and c

3. Health care professionals are often interested in being
   able to predict which patients are most likely to
   comply with medical recommendations. For example, it
   may be helpful to know in advance whether or not a
   hypertensive patient will benefit from a behavioral
   program designed to improve disease management. Let us
   assume that without any screening procedure 60% of
   these patients are able to reduce their blood pressure
   following instruction. Unfortunately, only 50% of those
   persons interested in taking part in the program can be
   admitted. A newly developed paper and pencil measure
   designed to evaluate the likelihood of medical
   compliance correlates .40 with actual patient adherence

(i.e. success). Use the table on page 182 of your text to determine the usefulness of this test. On the basis of this measure, the proportion of patients you would expect to be successful is:

a) 79%   d) 83%
b) 73%   e) 80%
c) 70%

4. A program similar to the one described above can only select 40 out of 100 patients. Using the same base rate for success and validity coefficient, approximately how many of the persons you select can be expected to fail?

a) 30
b) 28
c) 12
d) 10
e) 4

Thought Questions

1. Select a variable of interest that can be evaluated with some sort of test (i.e. medical, psychological, educational, etc.) and discuss the issues involved in determining an acceptable hit and miss rate. What would the base rate and cutting score be? What are the costs associated with false negatives and false positives? (pgs. 176-179)

_____
_____
_____
_____
_____
_____
_____
_____
_____
_____
_____
_____
_____
_____
_____
_____
_____
_____
_____
_____
_____
_____
_____
_____

2. Choose one of the reference books presented on pages
   188-190 and describe a test which it reviews. Try to
   evaluate your selection based on the principles
   discussed thus far in your text.

_____
_____
_____
_____
_____
_____
_____
_____
_____
_____
_____
_____
_____
_____
_____
_____
_____
_____
_____
_____
_____
_____
_____
_____
_____
_____
_____
_____
_____
_____
_____
_____
_____
_____

Answers

Terms, Concepts, and Names:

    cutting score (p.176)
    hit rate (p.176)
    base rate (p.176)
    false negatives (p.177)
    false positives (p.177)
    Taylor-Russel tables (p.180)
    utility theory (p.185)

incremental validity (p.186)
Tests in Print IV (p.188)
Mental Measurement Yearbook (p.189)

Fill-in Questions:

1. Standards for Educational and Psychological Testing
   (p.175)
2. reliability, validity, norms (p.175)
3. the proportion of cases in which a test accurately
   predicts success or failure (p.176)
4. base rate (p.176)
5. validity of the test, selection ratio (p.183)
6. dichotomous, utility theory (p.185)
7. incremental validity (p.187)

Multiple-Choice Questions:

1. d (p.176)
2. e (p.177)
3. b (p.182)
4. d (p.182-183); 75% of 40= 30; 40-30=10

Chapter 8

Test Administration

Terms, Concepts, and Names

Briefly identify the following:

expectancy effects_____
_____

Rosenthal effect_____
_____

reactivity_____
_____

drift_____
_____

contrast effect_____
_____

partial correlation_____
_____
_____

Fill-in Questions

1. Rosenthal asserted that expectancy effects are likely
   to result from subtle uses of _____
   between the experimenter and the subject.
2. It is important to give tests under
   _____ because situational variables can
   affect test scores.
3. Students with _____ often have
   difficulty focusing on test items and may be distracted
   by intrusive thoughts. This is an example of a
   _____.
4. An increase in the reliability of observers in
   behavioral observation studies is referred to as
   _____ and is a reaction to being checked.

Multiple-Choice Questions

1. In general, studies have indicated that the race of the

examiner
   a) should be the same as that of the subject
   b) should be different than that of the subject
   c) is not as important as sex of the examiner
   d) is only of importance with regard to intelligence
      tests
   e) is unrelated to test performance

2. Because reinforcement and feedback may damage the
   reliability and validity of test scores, most test
   manuals insist that
   a) feedback be given only by trained examiners
   b) no feedback be given
   c) feedback be given in a standardized manner
   d) feedback be given only if the subject appears to
      need encouragement
   e) feedback be given on a random basis

3. Which of the following is **not** an advantage of computer
   assisted test administration?
   a) performance dependent feedback
   b) patience
   c) control of bias
   d) excellence of standardization
   e) precision of timing responses

4. "Drift" refers to a problem inherent in the training of
   a) personality assessors
   b) intelligence testers
   c) test proctors
   d) behavioral observers
   e) computer-assisted test administrators

Thought Questions

1. The state of the subject may well affect his or her
   test performance and may be a serious source of error.
   Discuss some possible "subject variables" that may
   interfere with or improve an individual's performance
   on a test. (page 202-203)

_____
_____
_____
_____
_____
_____
_____
_____
_____
_____
_____

2. Explain some ways in which test administration can be
   standardized. (pages 199-203)

3. Integrity tests are widely used to predict the
integrity of potential employees. Discuss the controversy
surrounding this type of test. (page 205)_____

Answers

<u>Terms, Concepts, and Names</u>

      expectancy effects (p.196)
      Rosenthal effect (p.196)
      reactivity (p.203)
      drift (p.204)
      contrast effect (p.204)
      partial correlation (p.206)

<u>Fill-in Questions</u>

      1. nonverbal communication (p.197)
      2. standardized conditions (p.200)
      3. test anxiety, subject variable (p.202)
      4. reactivity (p.203)

<u>Multiple-Choice Questions</u>

      1. e (p.195)
      2. b (p.200)
      3. a (p.201)
      4. d (p.204)

Chapter 9

Interview Techniques

Terms, Concepts, and Names

Briefly identify the following:

social facilitation_____
_____

evaluative statements_____
_____

probing statements_____
_____

false reassurance_____
_____

open-ended question_____
_____

closed-ended question_____
_____

transitional phrase_____
_____

verbatim playback_____
_____

paraphrase_____
_____

clarification statement_____
_____

empathy response_____
_____

Carkhuff and Berenson_____
_____

active listening_____
_____

confrontation_____
_____
_____

SCID_____
_____
_____

mental status examination_____
_____
_____

halo effect_____
_____
_____

general standoutishness_____
_____
_____

Fill-in Questions

1. A study by Saccuzzo (1975) indicated that the patient's perceptions of the interviewer's _____ were the most important factor in the patient's evaluations of the quality of the interview.

2. _____ statements tend to put the interviewee on guard thus limiting his or her ease in revealing important information.

3. _____ statements demand more information than the interviewee is willing to provide voluntarily and should also be avoided. Many of these statements begin with _____ and tend to put the individual on the defensive.

4. The _____ response directs anger toward the interviewee.

5. _____ questions facilitate the interviewing process, while _____ questions bring the interview to a halt.

6. _____ and _____ help to keep the interview flowing and are interchangeable with the inetrviewee's response.

7. A powerful response that communicates that the interviewer understands how the interviewee must feel is the _____ response.

8. A confrontation response is used most appropriately in a(n)_____ interview.

9. The _____ interview often involves a search for negative or unfavorable evidence about the person.

10. The reliability of interview data centers around _____.

Multiple-Choice Questions

1. "Don't worry everything will be alright" is an example of
   a) an empathic response
   b) a facilitative response
   c) a confrontive response
   d) an effective response
   e) a response to be avoided

2. What two types of statements go just beyond the interviewee's response?
   a) clarification and transition
   b) clarification and summarizing
   c) clarification and verbatim playback
   d) summarizing and paraphrasing
   e) paraphrasing and restatement

3. Within Carkhuff and Berenson's 5-point system, what is the minimum level of responding necessary to facilitate an interaction?
   a) III
   b) I
   c) II
   d) V
   e) all of the above

4. A special type of interview used primarily to diagnose psychosis, brain damage, and other major mental health problems is the
   a) evaluation interview
   b) assessment interview
   c) case history interview
   d) mental status exam
   e) employment interview

Thought Questions

1. Describe the 5-point system of Carkhuff and Berenson which represents varying degrees of empathy, and provide examples of each response level. (pages 230-232)

_____
_____
_____
_____
_____
_____
_____

_____
_____
_____
_____
_____
_____
_____
_____
_____
_____
_____
_____
_____
_____

2. Discuss potential cross-ethnic, cross-cultural, and
   cross-class factors that may affect interview validity.
   How would you handle such an interview? (page 243)

_____
_____
_____
_____
_____
_____
_____
_____
_____
_____
_____
_____
_____
_____
_____
_____
_____
_____
_____

Answers

Terms, Concepts, and Names

social facilitation (p.222)
evaluative statements (p.224)
probing statements (p.224)
false reassurance (p.225)
open-ended question (p.225)
closed-ended question (p.225)
transitional phrase (p.226)
verbatim playback (p.227)
paraphrase (p.227)
clarification statement (p.227)
empathy response (p.228)
Carkhuff and Berenson (p.231)
active listening (p.232)
confrontation (p.232)
SCID (p.233)
mental status examination (p.238)
halo effect (p.242)
general standoutishness (p.242)

Fill-in Questions

1. feelings (p.223)
2. judgemental/evaluative (p.224)
3. probing, why (p.224)
4. hostile (p.224)
5. open-ended, closed-ended (p.225)
6. paraphrase, restatement (p.227)
7. empathy/understanding (p.228)
8. therapeutic (p.232)
9. employment (p.240)
10. interinterviewer agreement (p.244)

Multiple-Choice Questions

1. e (p.225)
2. b (p.227)
3. a (p.231)
4. d (p.238)

Chapter 10

Tests of Mental Ability: The Binet Scale

Terms, Concepts, and Names

Briefly identify the following:

age differentiation_____

_____

general mental ability_____

_____

Spearman's g_____

_____

positive manifold_____

_____

1905 Binet-Simon Scale_____

_____

1908 Binet-Simon Scale_____

_____

mental age_____

_____

L. M. Terman_____

_____

1916 Stanford-Binet Scale_____

_____

intelligence quotient (IQ)_____

_____

1937 Stanford-Binet Scale_____

_____

1960 Stanford-Binet Scale_____

_____

deviation IQ_____

_____

The Modern Binet Scale_____

_____

_____

primary mental abilities_____
_____
_____
basal_____
_____
_____
ceiling_____
_____
_____

Fill-in Questions

1. Rather than attempting to measure separate distinct abilities, Alfred Binet restricted his task to the measurement of _____.
2. The terms _____, _____, and _____ were used to designate levels of mental deficiency in the early versions of the Binet Scale.
3. The 1908 Scale retained and expanded upon the principle of age differentiation and was a(n) _____ scale.
4. Although the standardization sample of the 1916 Scale was markedly increased it was not _____.
5. If an eight year old child has a mental age of ten his or her IQ would be computed to be _____.
6. The most important improvement in the 1937 Scale was the inclusion of a(n) _____.
7. The single most significant psychometric problem of the 1937 Scale was the differential variability in IQ scores as a function of _____ _____.
8. In 1960, the _____ concept replaced the original IQ concept and is a standard score with a mean of _____ and a standard deviation of _____.
9. Unlike previous normative samples, the 1972 revised norms included _____.
10. The test format of the Modern (1986) Binet is _____, meaning that each individual is tested with a range of tasks best suited to his or her ability.

Multiple-Choice Questions

1. Binet's definition of intelligence combined one's capacity to (1) find and maintain a definite direction and purpose, (2) make adaptations if necessary to achieve that purpose, and (3)
   a) reach one's goal
   b) evaluate or criticize the strategy so that necessary adjustments can be made
   c) teach one's strategies to others

d) be creative in choosing one's strategies
e) none of the above

2. The first version of what is now referred to as the Stanford-Binet, the Binet-Simon Scale, was developed in
   a) 1905
   b) 1904
   c) 1916
   d) 1927
   e) 1960

3. The 30 items in the Binet-Simon Scale were arranged
   a) according to type of task
   b) randomly to avoid ordering effects
   c) according to underlying ability tapped
   d) in an increasing order of difficulty
   e) none of the above

4. The 1916 Stanford-Binet was developed under the direction of
   a) T. Simon
   b) J. P. Herring
   c) F. Kuhlman
   d) R. M. Yerkes
   e) L. M. Terman

5. On the Modern Binet Scale, the point at which three out of four items within a test are missed is called the
   a) criterion
   b) mental age
   c) ceiling
   d) level of general capability
   e) floor

6. The formula for computing the intelligence quotient (IQ) is
   a) IQ= Chronological age/Mental age x 100 (IQ=CA/MA x 100)
   b) IQ= Basal age/Mental age x 100 (IQ=BA/MA x 100)
   c) IQ= 100/Chronological age x Mental age (IQ=100/CA x MA)
   d) IQ= Mental age/Chronological age x 100 (IQ=MA/CA x 100)
   e) IQ= Chronological age/Basal age x 100 (IQ=CA/BA x 100)

7. A major problem with the Modern Binet is
   a) inadequate documentation of validity
   b) cumbersome administration
   c) poor overall reliability
   d) a small standardization sample
   e) norms that do not include ethnic minorities

Thought Questions

1. What was the initial impetus for the development of the Stanford-Binet Intelligence Scale? Are intelligence tests still used for this purpose? Describe other possible uses for tests such as the Binet in contemporary society. (pgs. 249-250)

_____
_____
_____
_____
_____
_____
_____
_____
_____
_____
_____
_____
_____
_____
_____
_____

2. Discuss the 3-level hierarchical model of the Modern Binet and compare it to Spearman's concept of general mental ability.   (pages 252-261)

_____
_____
_____
_____
_____
_____
_____
_____
_____
_____
_____
_____
_____
_____
_____
_____
_____

Terms, Concepts, and Names

age differentiation (p.250)
general mental ability (p.251)
Spearman's g (p.251)
positive manifold (p.251)
1905 Binet-Simon Scale (p.252)
1908 Binet-Simon Scale (p.253)
mental age (p.255)
L. M. Terman (p.255)
1916 Stanford-Binet Scale (p.256)
intelligence quotient (p.256)
1937 Scale (p.257)
1960 Scale (p.259)
deviation IQ (p.260)
Modern Binet Scale (p.261)
primary mental abilities (p.263)
basal (p.264)
ceiling (p.264)

Fill-in Questions

1. general mental ability (p.251)
2. idiot, imbecile, moron (p.253)
3. age (p.253)
4. representative (p.256)
5. 125 (p.257)
6. alternate equivalent form (p.257)
7. age of subject (p.258)
8. deviation IQ, 100, 16 (p.260)
9. non-whites (p.260)
10. adaptive (p.264)

Multiple-Choice Questions

1. b (p.248)
2. a (p.252)
3. d (p.253)
4. e (p.255)
5. c (p.264)
6. d (p.257)
7. b (p.269)

Chapter 11

The Wechsler Intelligence Scales

Terms, Concepts, and Names

Briefly identify the following:

point scale_____

_____

performance scale_____

_____

Wechsler Adult Intelligence Scale (WAIS-III)_____

_____

verbal subtests_____

_____

scaled score_____

_____

performance subtests_____

_____

pattern analysis_____

_____

Wechsler Intelligence Scale for Children, 3rd ed.
(WISC-III) _____

_____

Wechsler Preschool and Primary Scale of Intelligence-
Revised (WPPSI-R)_____

_____

_____

Fill-in Questions

1. Two major criticisms of the Binet Scale made by
   Wechsler (1939) were _____
   _____.
2. An important difference between the Wechsler and Binet
   scales is that the Binet employs a(n) _____
   concept while the Wechsler tests use a(n)
   _____ concept.
3. In a point scale credits or points are assigned to each
   item and items can be grouped together according to
   _____.

4. While Binet set out to measure the concept of general mental ability, Wechsler made an effort to measure _____.

5. The _____ subtest taps one of the most stable and best single measures of intelligence.

6. Raw scores on the WAIS-III subtests are converted into scaled scores with a mean of _____ and a standard deviation of _____.

7. To obtain a verbal IQ the _____ from each of the verbal subtests are summed and this sum is compared to _____.

8. _____ are supplementary subtests found on the Wechsler Intelligence Scale for Children, 3rd ed. (WISC-III) but not on the Wechsler Adult Intelligence Scale-III (WAIS-III).

9. The Wechsler Preschool and Primary Scale of Intelligence-R (WPPSI-R) measures intelligence in individuals from _____ to _____ years old.

10. The three unique subtests included in the WPPSI-R are _____, _____, and _____.

Multiple-Choice Questions

1. The main reason for including a performance scale in a measure of intelligence is to
   a) facilitate scoring
   b) increase ease of administration
   c) improve examiner-examinee rapport
   d) overcome language, cultural, and educational factors
   e) assist the examiner in determining the appropriate level at which to begin testing

2. Which of the following is **not** one of the WAIS-III performance scales
   a) object assembly
   b) block design
   c) arithmetic
   d) picture completion
   e) digit symbol

3. The major function measured by the comprehension subtest is
   a) judgement
   b) memory
   c) abstract thinking
   d) range of knowledge
   e) concentration

4. Alertness to details is best measured by the
   a) object assembly subtest
   b) picture completion subtest
   c) digit symbol subtest
   d) picture arrangement subtest
   e) similarities subtest

5. The performance IQ has a mean and standard deviation of
   a) 100, 15
   b) 10, 3
   c) 100, 10
   d) 100, 3
   e) 10, 5

6. One criticism of the WAIS-III is
   a) its weakness in measuring verbal abilities
   b) its poor reliability
   c) its poor validity
   d) its poor norms and standardization
   e) its weakness in measuring extreme IQs

7. Which of the following is **not** a weakness of the
   WISC-III
   a) poor split-half reliability coefficients for the
      verbal, performance, and full scale IQ scores
   b) it does not take into account more recent theories
      of multiple intelligences
   c) it lacks treatment validity for children with
      specific academic deficiencies
   d) it contains problems of bias for certain cultural
      and racial groups
   e) all of the above are weaknesses of the WISC-III

Thought Questions

1. Choose one of the WAIS-III subtests and discuss
   possible non-intellectual factors that may influence an
   individual's performance. (p.277-283)

   _____
   _____
   _____
   _____
   _____
   _____
   _____
   _____
   _____
   _____
   _____
   _____
   _____

_____
_____
_____
_____
_____
_____
_____
_____
_____
_____
_____
_____
_____

2. Describe some of the interpretive features of the
   WAIS-III.   (pgs. 284-289)

_____
_____
_____
_____
_____
_____
_____
_____
_____
_____
_____
_____
_____
_____
_____
_____
_____
_____
_____
_____
_____
_____
_____
_____
_____

Terms, Concepts and Names

      point scale (p.274)
      performance scale (p.274)
      Wechsler Adult Intelligence Scale-III (WAIS-III)
      (p.275)
      verbal subtests (pgs.277-280)
      scaled score (p.280)
      performance subtests (pgs.281-283)
      pattern analysis (p.286)
      Wechsler Intelligence Scale for Children, 3rd ed.
      (WISC-III) (p.292)
      Wechsler Preschool and Primary Scale of
      Intelligence-R (WPPSI-R) (p.298)

Fill-in Questions

1. use of a single score as a measure of intelligence; the inappropriateness of the Binet Scale as a measure of adult intelligence (pg.273)
2. age scale, point scale (p.273)
3. content (p.274)
4. separate interrelated abilities (p.277)
5. vocabulary (p.280)
6. 10, 3 (p.280)
7. scaled scores, the standardization sample for the individual's age group (p.281)
8. mazes and symbol search (p.292)
9. 4, 6 1/2 (p.298)
10. animal pegs, geometric design, sentences (p.298)

Multiple-Choice Questions

1. d (p.275)
2. c (p.281)
3. a (p.278)
4. b (p.281)
5. a (p.284)
6. e (p.292)
7. a (p.296)

Chapter 12

Other Individual Tests of Ability

Terms, Concepts, and Names

Briefly identify the following:

Seguin Form Board Test_____
_____

Brazelton Neonatal Assessment Scale_____
_____

Gesell Developmental Schedules_____
_____

developmental quotient_____
_____

Bayley Scales of Infant Development_____
_____

Cattell Infant Intelligence Scale_____
_____

McCarthy Scales of Children's Abilities_____
_____

general cognitive index_____
_____

Kaufman Assessment Battery for Children (K-ABC)_____
_____

Columbia Mental Maturity Scale_____
_____

age deviation score_____
_____

Peabody Picture Vocabulary Test-Revised_____
_____

Leiter International Performance Scale_____
_____

Porteus Maze Test_____
_____

Illinois Test of Psycholinguistic Abilities_____

_____
_____

human information processing_____

_____
_____

Woodcock-Johnson Psycho-Educational Battery_____

_____
_____

Benton Visual Retention Test_____

_____
_____

psychological deficit_____

_____
_____

Bender Visual Motor Gestalt Test_____

_____
_____

Memory for Designs Test_____

_____
_____

Torrance Tests of Creative Thinking_____

_____
_____

Wide Range Achievement Test-Revised_____

_____
_____

Fill-in Questions

1. Although usually weaker in terms of psychometric
   properties, many of the alternatives to the major
   scales are not as reliant on a(n) _____ as are the
   Binet and Wechsler Scales.
2. The Seguin Form Board Test was used primarily
   to_____ and emphasized_____.
3. The major limitation of the Brazelton Scale is
   _____.
4. The Bayley Scale produces to main scores: _____
   and _____.
5. The _____ was designed as a downward
   extension of the Stanford-Binet.
6. The _____ yield(s) a composite score known
   as the general cognitive index.
7. The Kaufman Assessment Battery for Children (K-ABC) is
   based on a combination of several theoretical
   approaches including Luria's neuropsychological model
   of brain functioning, the theory of split brain
   functioning, and theories of _____.

8. One of the distinguishing characteristics of the Columbia Mental Maturity Scale is that it requires neither a(n) _____ nor _____.
9. The Peabody Picture Vocabulary Test purports to measure _____ which is presumed to be a nonverbal estimate of verbal intelligence.
10. The _____ is a test for individual's 2-18 years of age, can be administered without the use of language, and requires no verbal response from subjects.
11. The Illinois Test of Psycholinguistic Abilities assumes that a human response to an outside stimulus can be viewed in terms of discrete stages or processes. Stage 2 of processing involves _____ _____.
12. The idea behind the _____ is that a deficit on a visual memory task is consistent with possible brain damage.
13. Errors on the Bender Visual Motor Gestalt Test can occur for people whose mental age is less than 9, _____, and _____.

Multiple-Choice Questions

1. Which of the following is **not** a difference among the alternatives to the major scales?
    a) the degree of psychometric superiority as compared to the Wechsler or Binet Scales
    b) the age range
    c) the type of score that results
    d) the type of response required
    e) the amount of examiner skill and experience necessary for administration

2. The developmental quotient (DQ) is employed in the
    a) Brazelton Neonatal Assessment Scale
    b) Bayley Scales of Infant Development
    c) Gesell Developmental Schedules
    d) Cattell Infant Intelligence Scale
    e) Kaufman Assessment Battery for Children

3. The developmental quotient (DQ) parallels the
    a) chrononlogical age (CA) concept
    b) intelligence quotient (IQ) concept
    c) general cognitive index (GCI) concept
    d) mental age (MA) concept
    e) age deviation score (ADS) concept

4. Which of the following tests seems to be a good
   predictor for handicapped populations but does not
   predict future intelligence within the normal ranges?
   a) Bayley Scales of Infant Development
   b) Cattell Infant Intelligence Scale
   c) Gesell Developmental Schedules
   d) Brazelton Neonatal Assessment Scale
   e) McCarthy Scales of Children's Abilities

5. The greatest difficulty with the Columbia Mental
   Maturity Scale in its present form is its
   a) poor standardization sample
   b) high vulnerability to random error
   c) poor test-retest reliability
   d) poor internal consistency
   e) both a and b

6. Which of the following is a procedure with relevance
   for assessing brain damage?
   a) Leiter International Performance Scale
   b) Illinois Test of Psycholinguistic Abilities
   c) Porteus Maze Test
   d) Bender Visual Motor Gestalt Test
   e) Columbia Mental Maturity Scale

Thought Questions

1. Discuss the advantages and disavantages of the
   alternative individual ability tests as compared to the
   Wechsler and Stanford-Binet Scales. (pgs.302-305)

_____
_____
_____
_____
_____
_____
_____
_____
_____
_____
_____
_____
_____
_____
_____
_____
_____
_____
_____
_____

2. Utilize the brief description of information processing theory found on pages 324-325 of your text in providing examples of how deficits at each of the three stages may interfere with performance. Also, discuss how impairements in each of the sensory modalities (i.e. visual, auditory, tactile) may impair learning.

Answers

Terms, Concepts, and Names

Seguin Form Board Test (p.305)
Brazelton Neonatal Assessment Scale (p.306)
Gesell Developmental Schedules (p.307)
developmental quotient (DQ) (p.308)
Bayley Scales of Infant Development (p.309)
Cattell Infant Intelligence Scale (p.311)
McCarthy Scales of Childerns's Abilities (p.313)
general cognitive index (p.313)
Kaufman Assessment Battery for Children (K-ABC)
(p.316)
Columbia Mental Maturity Scale (p.319)
age deviation score (p.320)

Peabody Picture Vocabulary Test (p.321)
Leiter International Performance Scale (p.322)
Porteus Maze Test (p.323)
Illinois Test of Psycholinguistic Abilities (p.324)
human information processing (p.324)
Woodcock-Johnson Psycho-Educational Battery (p.326)
Benton Visual Retention Test (p.327)
psychological deficit (p.327)
Bender Visual Motor Gestalt Test (p.328)
Memory for Designs Test (p.328)
Torrance Tests of Creative Thinking (p.330)
Wide Range Achievement Test-Revised (p.330)

Fill-in Questions

1. verbal response (p.302)
2. evaluate mentally retarded adults, speed of performance (p.305)
3. lack of normative data (p.306)
4. mental, motor (p.309)
5. Cattell Infant Intelligence Scale (p.311)
6. McCarthy Scales of Children's Abilities (p.313)
7. information processing theory (p.316)
8. verbal response, fine motor skills (p.320)
9. receptive vocabulary (p.321)
10. Leiter International Performance Scale (p.322)
11. analyzing or processing input information (p.325)
12. Benton Visual Retention Test (p.327)
13. individuals with organicity, individuals with emotional problems (p.328)

Multiple-Choice Questions

1. a (p.302)
2. c (p.308)
3. d (p.308)
4. a (p.310)
5. b (p.320)
6. d (p.328)

Chapter 13

Group Ability Tests: Intelligence, Achievement, and Aptitude

Terms, Concepts, and Names

Briefly identify the following:

individual test_____
_____

group test_____
_____

Stanford Achievement Test_____
_____

Metropolitan Achievement Test_____
_____

Kuhlmann-Anderson Test (KAT)_____
_____

Henmon-Nelson Test (H-NT)_____
_____

Cognitive Abilities Test (COGAT)_____
_____

Scholastic Assessment Test (SAT-I)_____
_____

Cooperative School and College Ability Tests (SCAT)_____
_____

American College Test (ACT)_____
_____

Graduate Record Examination Aptitude Test (GRE)_____
_____

Miller Analogies Test (MAT)_____
_____

Law School Admissions Test (LSAT)_____
_____

Raven Progressive Matrices (RPM)_____
_____

Goodenough-Harris Drawing Test (G-HDT)_____
_____

IPAT Culture Fair Intelligence Test_____
_____

Wonderlic Personnel Test (WPT)_____
_____

General Aptitude Test Battery (GATB)_____
_____

Armed Services Vocational Aptitude Battery (ASVAB)_____
_____
_____

Fill-in Questions

1. Individual tests require a(n) _____ examiner for
   a(n) _____ subject. Group tests, on the other
   hand, can be administered to _____ at
   the same time by a(n) _____.
2. With _____ tests subjects record their own
   responses but with _____ tests the examiner scores
   the subject's response.
3. The _____ test provides three separate
   scores; Verbal, Quantitative, and Nonverbal.
4. The purpose of the _____ test is to
   provide a quick measure of general intelligence.
5. The SAT-I Reasoning Test consists of two parts:
   _____ and _____.
6. The major assumption of the SCAT is that _____
   _____.
7. The GRE contains a general section that produces
   _____, _____, and _____ scores.
8. The LSAT contains three types of problems: _____,
   _____, and _____.
9. The Raven Progressive Matrices was initially designed
   to assess military recriuts independently of
   _____.
10. Scoring of the Goodenough-Harris Drawing Test follows
    the principle of _____.
11. The Armed Services Vocational Aptitude Battery (ASVAB)
    uses _____ which involves presenting an item
    of known difficulty and then presenting either a more
    difficult or a less difficult item depending on whether
    the test taker is correct.

Multiple-Choice Questions

1. Which of the following is **not** an advantage of group tests?
   a) they are more cost-efficient
   b) they provide a greater wealth of information about the subject
   c) they require less professional time
   d) they require less skill in and training of examiners
   e) they can be scored more objectively

2. It is best to refer the subject for individual testing when
   a) he or she receives a low score
   b) there are wide discrepancies between a test score and other sources of data
   c) the test may not be valid
   d) both b and c
   e) all of the above

3. Unlike most multilevel batteries the Kuhlmann-Anderson Test
   a) is primarily nonverbal
   b) is for individuals from first thru twelfth grade
   c) has poor norms
   d) is difficult to administer
   e) all of the above

4. A major weakness of the SAT-I is its
   a) poor validity documentation
   b) poor predictive power in discriminating the grades of students who score in the middle ranges
   c) low reliability coefficients
   d) inadequate norms
   e) both c and d

5. A score of 600 on the verbal section of the GRE would mean that the individual scored
   a) at the mean
   b) one standard deviation below the mean
   c) one standard deviation above the mean
   d) two standard deviations above the mean
   e) two standard deviations below the mean

6. Although adequate psychometrically, both the Miller Analogies Test and the GRE have rather poor
   a) construct validity
   b) internal consistency
   c) test-retest reliability
   d) predictive validity
   e) face validity

79

7. A major advantage of the Raven Progressive Matrices Test is that it
   a) has better validity documentation than most group tests
   b) does not correlate with traditional tests such as the Wechsler or Binet Scales
   c) is predictive of creativity
   d) minimizes the effects of language and culture
   e) all of the above

Thought Questions

1. Discuss the differences between achievement, aptitude, and intelligence tests and give an example of each. (pgs. 339-340)

_____
_____
_____
_____
_____
_____
_____
_____
_____
_____
_____
_____
_____
_____
_____
_____
_____
_____
_____

2. Your text outlines both some of the advantages and disadvantages of using the GRE as a means for selecting graduate students. Discuss these arguments and provide your own additional comments regarding the use and misuse of the GRE as a selection device. (pages 350-356)

_____
_____
_____
_____
_____
_____
_____

_____
_____
_____
_____
_____
_____
_____
_____
_____
_____

3. As mentioned in your text, one purpose of nonverbal and
   performance tests is to remove factors related to
   cultural influences so that pure intelligence can be
   measured. Discuss the types of factors one would want
   to eliminate and the likelihood of being able to do so.
   (page 362)

_____
_____
_____
_____
_____
_____
_____
_____
_____
_____
_____
_____
_____
_____
_____
_____
_____
_____

Answers

Terms, Concepts, and Names

individual test (p.334)
group test (p.337)
Stanford Achievement Test (p.341)
Metropolitan Achievement Test (p.341)
Kuhlman-Anderson Test (KAT) (p.342)
Henmon-Nelson Test (H-NT) (p.344)
Cognitive Abilities Test (COGAT) (p.345)
Scholastic Assessment Test (SAT-I) (p.346)

Cooperative School and College Ability Tests (SCAT)
(p.347)
American College Test (ACT) (p.350)
Graduate Record Examination Aptitude Test (GRE)
(p.350)
Miller Analogies Test (MAT) (p.356)
Law Scool Admissions Test (LSAT) (p.356)
Raven Progressive Matrices (RPM) (p.359)
Goodenough-Harris Drawing Test (G-HDT) (p.361)
IPAT Culture Fair Intelligence Test (p.362)
Wonderlic Personnel Test (WPT) (p.363)
General Aptitude Test Battery (p.363)
Armed Services Vocational Aptitude Battery (ASVAB)
(p.365)

Fill-in Questions

1. single, single, more than one person, single
   examiner (p.334)
2. group, individual (pgs.334-335)
3. Cognitive Abilities Test (p.345)
4. Henmon-Nelson Test (p.344)
5. verbal reasoning, mathematical reasoning (p.346)
6. previous success in acquiring school-learned
   abilities can predict future success in acquiring
   such abilities (p.350)
7. verbal, quantitaive, analytic (p.351)
8. reading comprehension, logical reasoning, and
   analytical reasoning (p.357)
9. educational factors (p.360)
10. age differentiation (p.362)
11. adaptive testing (p.366)

Multiple-Choice Questions

1. b (p.338)
2. e (p.339)
3. a (p.342)
4. b (p.347)
5. c (p.351)
6. d (p.356)
7. d (p.360)

Chapter 14

Tests for Choosing Careers

Terms, Concepts, and Names

Briefly identify the following:

Strong Vocational Interest Blank (SVIB)_____
_____

Strong-Campbell Interest Inventory (SCII)_____
_____

Campbell Interest and Skill Survey (CISS)_____
_____

Kuder Occupational Interest Survey (KOIS)_____
_____

Jackson Vocational Interest Survey (JVIS)_____
_____

Minnesota Vocational Interest Inventory (MVII)_____
_____

Career Assessment Inventory (CAI)_____
_____

Self-Directed Search (SDS)_____
_____

Samuel Osipow_____
_____

Donald Super_____
_____

vocational maturity_____
_____

Anne Roe_____
_____

California Occupational Preference Syrvey (COPS)_____
_____

attribution theory_____
_____

social ecology_____

checklists_____

_____

critical incidents_____

_____

observation_____

_____

interviews_____

_____

questionnaires_____

_____

Template-Matching Technique_____

_____

Fill-in Questions

1. The Strong Vocational Interest Blank (SVIB) was created using the _____ approach to test construction.
2. In addition to suggesting which occupational group might be best suited to a test taker's interests, the Kuder Occupational Interest Survey (KOIS) may also provide direction with regard to_____ .
3. The _____ is designed for individuals who are not oriented toward college and emphasizes skilled and semi-skilled trades.
4. Because it was designed for non-professionally oriented adults and avoids both cultural and sex biases, the _____ has been considered the working person's Strong-Campbell Interest Inventory (SCII).
5. Vocational maturity refers to the correspondence between _____ and the _____ for that age period.
6. The _____ was developed to measure the characteristics described by Roe's theory including person versus nonperson orientation.
7. Attribution theorists posit that events in a person's environment can be caused by one of three sources: _____, _____, and _____ .
8. According to attribution theory, when we are observers making judgements about other people we use _____ explanations. On the other hand, when we are the actors

84

in a situation we explain our behavior in terms of
_____.

9. One of the most important areas in social ecology is the study of _____.

10. Information gathered through observation may be biased since people change their behavior when they know they are being watched. To avoid this problem the _____ method is sometimes used.

Multiple-Choice Questions

1. A major improvement of the Strong-Campbell Interst Inventory (SCII) over the Strong Vocational Interest Blank (SVIB) was/were
   a) an incorporation of a theoretical base
   b) an increase in test-retest reliability
   c) scales devoid of sex bias
   d) both a and b
   e) both a and c

2. Which of the following is **not** one of Holland's six personality factors incorporated into the Strong-Campbell Interest Inventory?
   a) Realistic
   b) Artistic
   c) Intuitive
   d) Social
   e) Enterprising

3. Which of the following is **not** a component of the CISS?
   a) orientation
   b) occupational
   c) school subject
   d) basic
   e) all of the above are components of the CISS

4. Both the Strong-Campbell Interest Inventory and the Kuder Occupational Interest Survey have been criticized because
   a) they emphasize professions that require college educations
   b) they are strongly sex biased
   c) their predictive validity is questionable
   d) their reliability documentation is poor
   e) interpretation of scores is difficult

5. A theory of career choice which states that individuals go through five developmental stages leading to vocational maturity was proposed by
   a) Donald Super

b) D. P. Campbell
c) Samuel Osipow
d) Anne Roe
e) E. K. Strong

6. A series of scales used to evaluate different environments was developed by
   a) Moos
   b) Roe
   c) Strong
   d) Barker
   e) none of the above

7. Which of the following methods of job analysis involves the observation of behaviors that differentiate successful from unsuccessful employees?
   a) checklists
   b) observation
   c) questionnaires
   d) critical incidents
   e) interviews

Thought Questions

1. Comment on sex bias in interest inventories as discussed in your text on page 383.

_____
_____
_____
_____
_____
_____
_____
_____
_____
_____
_____
_____
_____
_____
_____

2. Utilize the discussion of attribution theory found on pages 387-388 of your text to describe why a particular event in your environment took place or is taking place. This can be an event in which you are the "actor" or the "observer."

_____
_____
_____

_____
_____
_____
_____
_____
_____
_____
_____
_____
_____
_____
_____
_____
_____
_____
_____
_____
_____
_____
_____

3. Describe the characteristics of a behavioral setting of
   interest and include some of the "rules" which govern
   this particular setting. (page 389)

_____
_____
_____
_____
_____
_____
_____
_____
_____
_____
_____
_____
_____
_____
_____
_____
_____

4. Use Table 14-8 on page 390 of your text to describe the
   environment in which you will be taking an exam for
   this course.

_____
_____
_____
_____
_____
_____
_____

_____
_____
_____
_____
_____
_____
_____
_____
_____

Answers

Terms, Concepts, and Names

Strong Vocational Interest Blank (SVIB) (p.370)
Strong-Campbell Interest Inventory (SCII) (p.371)
Campbell Interest and Skill Inventory (CISS) (p.374)
Kuder Occupational Interest Survey (KOIS) (p.378)
Jackson Vocational Interest Survey (JVIS) (p.381)
Minnesota Vocational Interest Inventory (MVII)
(p.381)
Career Assessment Inventory (CAI) (p.381)
Self-Directed Search (SDS) (p.382)
Samuel Osipow (p.384)
Donald Super (p.385)
vocational maturity (p.385)
Anne Roe (p.385)
California Occupational Preference Survey (COPS)
(p.386)
attribution theory (p.387)
social ecology (p.388)
checklists (p.392)
critical incidents (p.393)
observation (p.393)
interviews (p.393)
questionnaires (p.393)
Template-Matching Technique (p.394)

Fill-in Questions

1. criterion-keying/criterion group (p.370)
2. selection of a college major (p.378)
3. Minnesota Vocational Interest Inventory (MVII)
   (p.381)
4. Career Assessment Invenory (CAI) (p.382)
5. vocational behavior, expected behavior (p.385)
6. California Occupational Preference Survey (COPS)
   (p.386)
7. persons, entities, times (p.387)
8. trait, situations (p.387)
9. behavioral settings (p.388)
10. participant observation (p.393)

Multiple-Choice Questions

1. e (p.371)
2. c (p.372)
3. c (p.374)
4. a (p.381)
5. a (p.385)
6. a (p.390)
7. d (p.393)

Chapter 15

Structured Personality Tests

Terms, Concepts, and Names

Briefly identify the following:

personality_____

_____

self-report questionnaire_____

_____

structured/objective method of personality assessment_____

_____

deductive strategies_____

_____

logical-content strategy_____

_____

theoretical strategy_____

_____

empirical strategies_____

_____

criterion group strategy_____

_____

factor analytic strategy_____

_____

Woodworth Personal Data Sheet_____

_____

Bell Adjustment Inventory_____

_____

Bernreuter Personality Inventory_____

_____

Mooney Problem Checklist_____

_____

Minnesota Multiphasic Personality Inventory (MMPI/MMPI-2)

_____

_____

_____

California Psychological Inventory (CPI)_____

_____

J. P. Guilford_____

_____

R. B. Cattell_____

_____

Sixteen Personality Factor Questionnaire (16PF)_____

_____

Edwards Personal Preference Schedule (EPPS)_____

_____

ipsative score_____

_____

Personality Research Form (PRF)_____

_____

Jackson Personality Inventory_____

_____

Myers-Briggs Type Indicator_____

_____

Millon Clinical Multiaxial Inventory (MCMI-II)_____

_____

NEO Personality Inventory_____

_____

_____

Fill-in Questions

1. The principal distinguishing characteristic of the
   logical-content strategy is that it assumes that the
   test item _____.
2. The theoretical approach attempts to create a
   _____ scale.
3. When employing the criterion group strategy, the first
   step is to determine which items discriminate the
   criterion and control groups. The next step is to
   _____ the scale.
4. Factor analysts analyze intercorrelations among items
   or tests in order to find the minimum number of areas
   of _____ to account for as much of the
   variability in the data as possible.

5. The purpose of the Woodworth Personal Data Sheet was to_____.
6. Items on the Mooney Problem Checklist are interpreted on the basis of _____.
7. The logical-content approach has been criticized because in assuming the face validity of test items one also assumes that the subject takes a normal approach to the test, _____, _____, and _____.
8. The main idea behind the MMPI was to_____ _____.
9. The _____ scale(s) of the MMPI provide information concerning the subject's approach to testing.
10. The _____ scale was designed to identify individuals who attempt to fake bad.
11. Using two-point codes and other configural patterns, _____ attempted to empirically determine the meaning of MMPI elevations.
12. Name two psychometric inadequacies of the MMPI. _____.
13. _____ is a response style which is a tendency to agree or to edorse an item as true.
14. Cattell, through a series of factor analyses, reduced personality traits to 16 basic dimensions which he called _____.
15. One major criticism of the factor analytic approach is _____.
16. Each score on any given set of tests or variables can be broken down into three components: _____, _____, and _____.
17. Ipsative scores present results in _____ rather than as absolute totals.
18. The EPPS, the PRF and the JPI were based on_____.
19. The Myers-Briggs Type Indicator is based on Carl Jung's theory of psychological types and determines which of the four ways of knowing the world people rely on. These modes are: _____, _____, _____, and _____.

Multiple-Choice Questions

1. The two deductive strategies of test construction are the
   a) logical content and rational approaches
   b) logical content and empirical approaches
   c) logical content and theoretical approaches
   d) empirical and rational approaches
   e) intuitive and rational approaches

2. The criterion group strategy is also known as the
   a) empirical strategy
   b) external strategy
   c) factor analytic strategy
   d) both a and b
   e) both b and c

3. The Bell Adjustment Inventory is an example of
   a) the theoretical approach
   b) the criterion group approach
   c) the empirical approach
   d) the logical-content approach
   e) the factor analytic approach

4. The reading ability required for the MMPI-2 is at least
   a) 5th grade
   b) 8th grade
   c) 6th grade
   d) 12th grade
   e) 4th grade

5. The original MMPI scales consisted of how many validity
   and clinical scales respectively?
   a) 3, 10
   b) 5, 10
   c) 10, 10
   d) 5, 15
   e) 4, 10

6. Raw scores on the MMPI are converted to standardized
   scores called
   a) Z-scores
   b) V-scores
   c) T-scores
   d) C-scores
   e) K-scores

7. Which MMPI scale was designed to detect pathological
   individuals who produce normal patterns because of
   defensiveness?
   a) L scale
   b) K scale
   c) F scale
   d) Si scale
   e) D scale

8. The restandardization of the MMPI has eliminated the
   most serious drawback of the original version, namely
   a) an inadequate control group
   b) lack of validity documentation
   c) poor reliability
   d) inter-item correlations

e) poor predictive ability for certain ethnic groups

9. A number of studies have indicated that the MMPI might be useful in the early detection of individuals who later become
   a) rapists
   b) child molesters
   c) physically ill
   d) obese
   e) alcoholics

10. The advantage of the CPI over the MMPI is that
    a) there is no intercorrelation among scales
    b) it can be used with normal subjects
    c) true-false keying is balanced to prevent response bias
    d) reliability coefficients are impressive
    e) criterion groups were carefully and accurately selected

11. The EPPS exemplifies which of the following approaches to test construction?
    a) the factor analytic strategy
    b) the criterion group strategy
    c) the criterion-keying method
    d) the logical-content approach
    e) the theoretical strategy

12. Which of the following tests is characterized by a forced-choice format?
    a) EPPS
    b) 16PF
    c) CPI
    d) MMPI
    e) PRF

13. The purpose of which of the following tests is to help make a diagnosis on Axis II of the DSM-IIIR?
    a) NEO Personality Inventory
    b) Myers-Briggs Type Indicator
    c) MCMI-II
    d) CPI
    e) JPI

Thought Questions

1. Select one of the approaches to test construction described on pages 400-404 of your text and discuss both the advantages and disadvantages of this strategy for personality test construction. What modifications

might you make to improve on this approach?

_____
_____
_____
_____
_____
_____
_____
_____
_____
_____
_____
_____
_____
_____
_____
_____

2. The measurement of personality assumes that humans possess characteristics or traits that are stable across situations, vary from individual to individual, and can be measured. Discuss these assertions and your agreement and/or disageement with them as well as possible alternative assumptions; for example, situational variables.

_____
_____
_____
_____
_____
_____
_____
_____
_____
_____
_____
_____
_____
_____
_____
_____
_____
_____
_____
_____
_____

Answers

<u>Terms, Concepts, and Names</u>

personality (p.399)
self-report questionnaire (p.400)
structured/objective method of personality assessment
(p.401)
deductive strategies (p.401)
logical-content strategy (p.401)
theoretical strategy (p.402)
empirical strategies (p.402)
criterion group strategy (p.402)
factor analytic strategy (p.403)
Woodworth Personal Data Sheet (p.404)
Bell Adjustment Inventory (p.405)
Bernreuter Personality Inventory (p.405)
Mooney Problem Checklist (p.405)
Minnesota Multiphasic Personality Inventory
(MMPI/MMPI-2) (p.407)
California Pychological Inventory (CPI) (p.417)
J. P. Guilford (p.419)
R. B. Cattell (p.420)
Sixteen Personality Factor Questionnaire (16PF)
(p.420)
Edwards Personal Preference Schedule (EPPS) (p.423)
ipsative score (p.425)
Personality Research Form (PRF) (p.426)
Jackson Personality Inventory (p.426)
Myers-Briggs Type Indicator (p.427)
Millon Clinical Multiaxial Inventory (MCMI-II)
(p.430)
NEO Personality Inventory (p.431)

<u>Fill-in Questions</u>

1. describes the subject's personality and behavior
   (p.402)
2. homogenous (p.402)
3. cross-validate (p.403)
4. common variance (p.404)
5. identify military recruits likely to break down in
   combat (p.405)
6. face vailidity (p.406)
7. complies with instructions, reads each item,
   answers as honestly as possible (p.406)
8. assume nothing about the meaning of a subject's
   response to a test item (p.406)
9. validity (p.410)
10. F Scale (p.411)

11. Paul Meehl (p.412)
12. any two of the following: composition of scales,
    intercorrelations among the scales, imbalance in
    the way items are keyed, relationship of
    demographic characteristics to scales (p.415-417)
13. Acquiescence (p.416)
14. source traits (p.420)
15. the subjective nature of the process of naming
    factors (p.422)
16. common variance, unique variance, error variance
    (p.422)
17. relative terms (p.425)
18. Murray's (1938) theory of needs (p.426)
19. sensing, intuition, feeling, thinking (p.427-428)

Multiple-Choice Questions

1. c (p.402)
2. d (p.402)
3. d (p.405)
4. b (p.407)
5. a (p.413)
6. c (p.411)
7. b (p.411)
8. a (p.417)
9. e (p.417)
10. b (p.417)
11. e (p.423)
12. a (p.423)
13. c (p.430)

Chapter 16
Projective Personality Tests

Terms, Concepts, and Names

Briefly identify the following:

projective hypothesis_____

_____

Rorschach Inkblot Test_____

_____

Psychodiagnostik_____

_____

administration of the Rorschach_____

_____

scoring of the Rorschach_____

_____

Holtzman Inkblot Test_____

_____

Thematic Apperception Test (TAT)_____

_____

Southern-Mississippi TAT (SM-TAT)_____

_____

Children's Apperception Test (CAT)_____

_____

Gerontological Apperception Test_____

_____

Word Association Test_____

_____

Rotter Incomplete Sentence Blank_____

_____

Figure Drawing Tests_____

_____

_____

Fill-in Questions

1. The projective hypothesis proposes that an individual's interpretation of _____ stimuli tends to reflect his or her _____.

2. Although inkblots had been used previously for a variety of purposes Herman Rorschach found an original and important use for inkblots; _____.

3. Exner (1974) advocates an administration procedure in which the examiner sits next to the subject rather than face to face in order to prevent the examiner from

_____.

4. The two phases of Rorschach adminstration are the _____ phase and the _____.

5. In scoring for location, a _____ response indicates that the subject overgeneralized from a part to the whole.

6. Four of the properties of an inkblot that may determine or lead to a response are _____, _____, _____, and _____.

7. "Populars" are responses that occur _____.

8. The specific content of Rorschach responses and an analysis of the sequence of responses are examples of _____ aspects of scoring.

9. Two factors that contribute to the problem of evaluating the psychometric properties of the Rorschach are _____ and

_____.

10. Although it possesses psychometric advantages over the Rorschach, the main problem with the Hotzman Inkblot Test appears to be its _____.

11. While the Rorschach is basically atheoretical, the Thematic Apperception Test (TAT) is based on

_____.

12. Almost all methods of TAT interpretation take into account _____, _____, _____, _____, and _____.

Multiple-Choice Questions

1. Which of the following is **not** one of the five individuals who originally played a dominant role in the use and investigation of the Rorschach?
    a) Beck
    b) Hertz
    c) Klopfer
    d) Exner
    e) Piotrowski

2. How many Rorschach Inkblot cards are there?
   a) 15
   b) 10
   c) 5
   d) 20
   e) 12

3. The purpose of the second phase of Rorschach administration, the inquiry, is to
   a) determine how long it takes a subject to respond to a card
   b) record the position of the card when the response is made
   c) allow the examiner to score the response
   d) check the reliability of the subject's response
   e) both a and b

4. Form quality is a scoring dimension which refers to
   a) where the pereception was seen
   b) what determined the response
   c) the extent to which the response matched the stimulus properties of the inkblot
   d) the extent to which the response was unique
   e) what the perception was

5. A comprehensive system for administering and scoring the Rorschach was developed by
   a) Beck
   b) Hertz
   c) Klopfer
   d) Exner
   e) Piotrowski

6. In TAT interpretation the environmental forces that interfere with or facilitate the satisfaction of various needs are called
   a) press
   b) external stimuli
   c) themes
   d) determinors
   e) stressors

7. A number of assumptions for TAT interpretation were analyzed by
   a) Morgan
   b) Murray
   c) Bellack
   d) Lindzey
   e) Murstein

8. One problem with Figure Drawing Tests is that
    a) they can only be used with children
    b) they are difficult to administer
    c) there is a tendency to overinterpret the test data
    d) there is no standard scoring method
    e) both c and d

Thought Questions

1. A summary of arguments for and against the Rorschach is presented in Table 16-2 on page 449 of your text. Discuss these arguments and include your own views regarding the utility of the Rorschach Inkblot Test.

_____
_____
_____
_____
_____
_____
_____
_____
_____
_____
_____
_____
_____
_____
_____
_____
_____
_____

2. Discuss the similarities and differences between the Rorschach Inkblot Test and TAT. (see Table 16-3 on page 452)

_____
_____
_____
_____
_____
_____
_____
_____
_____
_____
_____
_____
_____

Terms, Concepts, and Names

projective hypothesis (p.437)
Rorschach Inkblot Test (p.438)
Psychodiagnostik (p.439)
Rorschach administration (pgs.439-441)
Rorschach scoring (pgs.441-445)
Holtzman Inkblot Test (p.451)
Thematic Apperception Test (TAT) (p.451)
Southern-Mississippi TAT (SM-TAT) (p.457)
Children's Apperception Test (CAT) (p.457)
Gerontological Apperception Test (p.457)
Word Association Test (p.458)
Rotter Incomplete Sentence Blank (p.459)
Figure Drawing Tests (p.459)

Fill-in Questions

1. vague/ambiguous; needs, feelings, experiences, prior conditioning, thought processes, etc. (p.437)
2. identifying psychological disorders (p.439)
3. inadvertently revealing information or reinforcing certain types of responses through facial expressions or nonverbal communication (p.440)
4. free association, inquiry (p.440)
5. confabulatory (p.441)
6. form, movement, color, shading (p.442)
7. once in three protocols (p.444)
8. qualitative (p.444)
9. lack of a standard method of administration, lack of standard scoring procedures (p.448)
10. validity (p.451)
11. Murray's (1938) theory of needs (p.451)
12. hero, needs, press, themes, outcomes (p.454)

Multiple-Choice Questions

1. d (p.439)
2. b (p.439)
3. c (p.441)
4. c (p.444)
5. d (p.450)
6. a (p.454)
7. d (p.455)
8. e (p.460)

Chapter 17

Alternatives to Traditional Psychological Tests

Terms, Concepts, and Names

Briefly identify the following:

medical model_____

_____

behavioral assessment_____

_____

operant conditioning_____

_____

baseline_____

_____

behavioral excesses and deficits_____

_____

self-report techniques_____

_____

Fear Survey Schedule (FSS)_____

_____

Assertive Behavior Survey Schedule (ABSS)_____

_____

Rathus Assertiveness Schedule (RAS)_____

_____

Conflict Resolution Inventory (CRI)_____

_____

self-report battery_____

_____

Kanfer and Saslow's functional approach_____

_____

cognitive-behavioral assessment_____

_____

Dysfunctional Attitude Scale (DAS)_____

_____

Irrational Beliefs Test (IBT)_____
_____
_____
Michenbaum_____
_____
_____
cognitive functional analysis_____
_____
_____
psychophysiological assessment_____
_____
_____
Ax_____
_____
_____
artifacts_____
_____
_____
psychophysical and signal detection procedures_____
_____
_____
Saccuzzo_____
_____
_____
iconic storage_____
_____
_____

Fill-in Questions

1. The medical model assumes that overt manifestations of psychopathology are only _____ of a(n) _____ cause.
2. In behavioral assessment the _____ is(are) considered the real problem.
3. The first step in behavioral assessment based on operant conditioning is to _____.
4. The establishment of a baseline involves an evaluation of the _____, _____ or _____ of the critical response(s).
5. In behavioral terms overeating is an example of a behavioral _____ while undereating is an example of a behavioral _____.
6. An individual's responses to self-report items are assumed to be related to _____.
7. Behavioral self-report procedures focus on _____ that lead to particular response patterns. Traditional procedures, on the other hand, focus on _____ _____ that lead to particular

104

response patterns.

8. Both early and present-day self-report procedures assume that a test response can be interpreted on the basis of _____.

9. The focus of Kanfer and Salslow's functional approach is on _____ and _____.

10. Thought sampling, assessing imagery, assessing beliefs, and assessing self-statements are all examples of _____.

11. The premise underlying _____ is that what an individual says to his or herself plays an important role in behavior.

12. Mechanical counters attached to the jaw that record the number of bites taken while eating and electronic devices attached to cigarette cases which count the number of times it is opened, are examples of _____.

13. Saccuzzo and his colleagues have attempted to demonstrate that _____ may be evaluated by psychophysical methods.

Multiple-Choice Questions

1. The Fear Survey Schedule (FSS) attempts to identify
   a) those individuals most likely to be fearful in a variety of situations
   b) internal characteristics that lead to fear responses
   c) situations that elicit fear and avoidance
   d) how fearful individuals are of a variety of phenomena
   e) the circumstances under which typically fearful individuals are the least likely to be afraid

2. Which of the following questionnaires seeks to determine whether or not an individual would comply with a series of unreasonable requests and how he or she would feel about his or her response?
   a) Conflict Resolution Inventory (CRI)
   b) Assertive Behavior Survey Schedule (ABSS)
   c) Fear of Negative Evaluation Scale (FNE)
   d) Rathus Assertiveness Schedule (RAS)
   e) Social Avoidance Distress Scale (SAD)

3. A strength of the Fear Survey Schedule (FSS) that sets it apart from other self-report techniques is its
   a) standardized administration procedure
   b) standardized scoring and interpreation
   c) generalizability to a variety of populations
   d) excellent test-retest reliability
   e) none of the above

4. Which of the following researchers in psychophysiological assessment demonstrated that the fear response was related to specific physiological changes?
   a) Klinger
   b) Michenbaum
   c) Powell
   d) Azrin
   e) Ax

5. One potential drawback of the computerization of traditional tests is that
   a) there is a significant reduction in reliability
   b) interpretations based on computre programs must be viewed with caution
   c) there are frequent scoring errors
   d) computerized test administration is cumbersome
   e) there is an apreciable decrease in validity

Thought Questions

1. A 40 year old woman has been drinking alcohol excessively for the past 15 years. Her behavior has recently caused her to be fired from her job and is starting to detrimentally affect her relationships with her husband and children. Discuss how you would assess and begin to treat her problem first from a traditional (medical model) perspective and then using an alternative assessment procedure. (pgs. 465-480)

_____
_____
_____
_____
_____
_____
_____
_____
_____
_____
_____
_____
_____

_____
_____
_____
_____
_____
_____

2. Choose a behavior that you would like to increase or
   decrease. For example, you may want to eat less,
   exercise more, increase your study time, or decrease
   your television watching. The steps outlined in Table
   17-3 on page 467 of your text may be helpful in
   planning an intervention. What rewards and/or
   punishments did you use? How effective was your
   intervention? The example on pages 467-469 may serve
   as a useful guideline.

_____
_____
_____
_____
_____
_____
_____
_____
_____
_____
_____
_____
_____
_____
_____
_____

Answers

Terms, Concepts, and Names

     medical model (p.465)
     behavioral assessment (p.466)
     operant conditioning (p.467)
     baseline (p.467)
     behavioral excesses and deficits (p.467)
     self-report techniques (p.467)
     Fear Survey Schedule (FSS) (p.470)
     Assertive Behavior Survey Shedule (ABSS) (p.472)

Rathus Assertiveness Schedule (RAS) (p.472)
Conflict Resolution Inventory (CRI) (p.472)
self-report battery (p.473)
Kanfer and Saslow's functional approach (p.474)
cognitive-behavioral assessment (p.475)
Dysfunctional Attitude Scale (DAS) (p.475)
Irrational Beliefs Test (IBT) (p.473)
Michenbaum (p.477)
cognitive functional analysis (p.477)
psychophysiological assessment (p.479)
Ax (p.479)
artifacts (p.480)
psychophysical and signal detection procedures
(p.480)
Saccuzzo (p.481)
iconic storage (p.481)

Fill-in Questions

1. symptom, underlying (p.465)
2. overt behaviors that define a disordered condition (p.466)
3. identify the critical response involved in the disorder (p.467)
4. frequency, intensity, duration (p.467)
5. excess, deficit (p.467)
6. behavior that can actually be observed (p.467)
7. situations, enduring internal characteristics of the individual (p.470)
8. face validity (p.473)
9. behavioral excesses, behavioral deicits (p.474)
10. cognitive-behavioral assessment (p.475)
11. cognitive functional analysis (p.476)
12. self-monitoring devices (p.478)
13. psychological disorders (p.481)

Multiple-Choice Questions

1. c (p.470)
2. a (p.472)
3. e (p.473)
4. e (p.479)
5. b (p.484)

Chapter 18

Measures of Anxiety and Stress

<u>Terms, Concepts and Names:</u>

<u>Briefly identify the following:</u>

stress_____
_____
_____

anxiety_____
_____

State-Trait Anxiety Inventory (STAI)_____
_____

Taylor Manifest Anxiety Scale_____
_____

Test Anxiety Questionnaire (TAQ)_____
_____

Test Anxiety Scale (TAS)_____
_____

Survey of Recent Events (SRE)_____
_____

Life Experiencs Survey (LES)_____
_____

Ways of Coping Scale_____
_____

Coping Inventory_____
_____

Ecological Momentary Assessment (EMA)_____
_____

Social Support_____
_____

Social Support Questionnaire (SSQ)_____
_____
_____

Fill-in Questions

1. The Life Experiences Survey (LES) yeilds two separate scores; one for _____ events, and one for _____ events, making this instrument different from other life change measures.
2. The Ways of Coping Scale includes seven subscales that can be divided into _____ or _____ strategies for dealing with stressful situations.
3. The Test Anxiety Questionnaire (TAQ) is based on test anxiety theory which distinguishes between two different drives or motivational states that operate in test taking situations; _____ and _____.
4. The focus of the test anxiety problem in the Test Anxiety Questionnaire (TAQ) is the _____ and in the Test Anxiety Scale (TAS) the _____.
5. An advantage of the EMA is that the information is collected in _____.

Multiple-Choice Questions

1. Which of the following change events has the highest life change unit (LCU) value?
   a) detention in jail
   b) divorce
   c) change in residence
   d) death of a close family member
   e) being fired from work

2. Which of the following constructs is not typically included in the definition of social support?
   a) financial assistance
   b) encouragement
   c) physical aid
   d) current life stress
   e) all of the above are included

3. The Taylor Manifest Anxiety Scale was created by selecting items that describe anxiety states from which of the following tests?
   a) EPPS
   b) 16PF
   c) CPI
   d) MMPI
   e) Mooney Problem Checklist

Thought Questions

1. Discuss the relationship between life stress and physical illness. (pages 497-499).

_____

_____

_____

_____

_____

_____

_____

_____

_____

_____

_____

_____

_____

_____

_____

_____

_____

2. Using either a systematic desensitization or cognitive-behavior modification approach, describe how you might decrease your own level of test anxiety. (page 496)

_____

_____

_____

_____

_____

_____

_____

_____

_____

_____

_____

_____

_____

_____

_____

_____

_____

Terms, Concepts, and Names

stress (p.487)
anxiety (p.488)
State-Trait Anxiety Inventory (STAI) (p.488)
Taylor Manifest Anxiety Scale (p.490)
Test Anxiety Questionnaire (TAQ) (p.492)
Test Anxiety Scale (TAS) (p.493)
Survey of Recent Events (SRE) (p.497)
Life Change Unit (LCU) (p.497-498)
Life Experiences Survey (LES) (p.500)
Ways of Coping Scale (p.501)
Coping Inventory (p.502)
Ecological Momentary Assessment (EMA) (p.502)
Social Support (p.503)
Social Support Questionnaire (SSQ) (p.504)

Fill-in Questions

1. positive, negative (p.500)
2. problem-focused, emotion-focused (p.501)
3. learned task drive;   learned anxiety drive (p.492)
4. situation;   person (p.494)
5. the subject's natural environment (p.502)

Multiple-choice Questions

1. b (p.498)
2. d (p.503)
3. d (p.490)

Chapter 19

Testing in Health Care Settings

Terms, Concepts, and Names

Briefly identify the following:

Clinical neuropsychology_____
_____

Learning Disability_____
_____

Halsted-Reitan Test Battery_____
_____

Luria-Nebraska Inventory_____
_____

pluripotentiality_____
_____

California Verbal Learning Test (CVLT and CVLT-C)_____
_____

quality-of-life-assessment_____
_____

health status_____
_____

psychometric approach to quality-of-life-assessment_____
_____

decision theory approach to quality-of-life-assessment_____
_____

Sickness Impact Profile (SIP)_____
_____

Index of Activities of Daily Living (ADL)_____
_____

Karnofsky Performance Status (KPS)_____
_____

McMaster Health Index Questionnaire (MHIQ)_____
_____

SF-36_____

_____

Nottingham Health Profile (NHP)_____

_____

Quality Adjusted Life Years (QALY)_____

_____

_____

Fill-in Questions

1. Clinical neuropsychology is a multi-disciplinary endeavor which overlaps with _____, _____ and _____.
2. _____ is an example of a learning disorder characterized by reading backwards.
3. The major emphasis of the _____ is to determine how errors are made in learning tasks.
4. One way to evaluate the health status of nations is in terms of their _____.
5. According to the WHO definition of health status, "health is a complete state of _____, _____ and _____ well-being, and not merely the absence of disease."
6. The two major approaches to quality of life assessment are _____ and _____ _____.
7. The Sickness Impact Profile (SIP) is divided into three major clusters of items: _____ _____, _____, and _____.
8. The _____ is the most commonly used instrument to assess health in the elderly.
9. The Karnofsky Performance Status (KPS) has been used widely in _____ research.
10. The goal of the multi-disciplinary group of specialists who created the McMaster Health Index Questionnaire (MHIQ) was to develop an instrument that conforms with _____.
11. Quality adjusted life years take into consideration the _____ consequences of various illnesses.
12. The approach to quality adjusted life years assessment described in this chapter classifies patients according to objective levels of functioning. These levels are represented by scales of _____, _____ and _____.

Multiple-Choice Questions

1. Most of the work in neuropsychology is directed toward the assessment of
   a) sensations/perceptions
   b) brain dysfunction
   c) mood
   d) motor movements
   e) learning

2. An important characteristic that specifically identifies the decision theory approach to quality of life assessment is that
   a) it provides separate measures for different dimensions of quality of life
   b) it asks respondents to choose from alternatives to determine what their quality of life is
   c) it is based upon subjective ratings by physicians
   d) it attempts to weight different dimensions of health
   e) all of the above

3. Scores on which of the following test(s) can be plotted on a graphic display similar to an MMPI profile
   a) Sickness Impact Profile (SIP)
   b) Rand Health Insurance Measure
   c) McMaster Health Index Questionnaire (MHIQ)
   d) Index of Activities of Daily Living Scale (ADL)
   e) Karnofsky Performance Status (KPS)

4. A criticism of the Activities of Daily Living Scale (ADL) is that
   a) there is no documentation of validity
   b) it does not distinguish adequately between individuals who are at the well end of the quality of life continuum
   c) it is scored in too subjective a manner
   d) there are inadequate norms
   e) most persons obtain very low scores on the scale decreasing its utility for research

5. In cost/utility analysis, observable health states are weighted by
   a) utility judgments of quality
   b) an individual's level of productivity
   c) length of illness
   d) health care costs
   e) extent of treatment needed

Thought Questions

1. Discuss how an evaluation of quality of life contributes to our conceptualization of health status (pgs.520-522).

_____
_____
_____
_____
_____
_____
_____
_____
_____
_____
_____
_____
_____
_____
_____
_____
_____
_____
_____
_____
_____
_____

2. Discuss some of the implications of the WHO's expanded definition of health (p.521).

_____
_____
_____
_____
_____
_____
_____
_____
_____
_____
_____
_____
_____
_____
_____
_____
_____
_____

3. Describe the difficulty that is likely to be encountered when a researcher attempts to measure a relationship between variables with instruments that have low reliability. <u>Note:</u> it may be helpful to use a specific example (p.528).

_____
_____
_____
_____
_____
_____
_____
_____
_____
_____
_____
_____
_____
_____
_____
_____
_____
_____
_____
_____

ANSWERS

Terms, Concepts, and Names

Clinical neuropsychology (p.508)
Learning Disability (p.510)
Halstead Reitan (p.513)
Luria Nebraska (p.513)
pluripotentiality (p.514)
California Verbal Learning Test (CVLT/CVLT-C) (p.517)
Quality of Life Assessment (p.520)
health status (p.521)
psychometric approach (p.521)
decision theory approach (p.521)
Sickness Impact Profile (SIP) (p.522)
Index of Activities of Daily Living (ADL) (p.524)
Karnofsky Performance Status (KPS) (p.526)
McMaster Health Index Questionnaire (MHIQ) (p.527)
SF-36 (p.528)
Nottingham Health Profile (NHP) (p.528)
quality adjusted life years (QALY) (p.529)

Fill-in Questions

1. neurology, psychiatry, psychometric testing (p.509)
2. Dyslexia (p.510)
3. California Verbal Learning Test (CVLT) (p.517)
4. infant mortality (p.520)
5. physical, mental, and social (p.521)
6. psychometric, decision theory (p.521)
7. Independent categories, physical, psychosocial (p.522)
8. Activities of Daily Living (ADL) (p.524)
9. cancer (p.526)
10. WHO definition of health (p.527)
11. quality-of-life (p.529)
12. mobility, physical activity, and social activity (p.530)

Multiple-Choice Questions

1. b (p.509)
2. d (p.521)
3. a (p.522)
4. b (p.524)
5. a (p.530)

Chapter 20

Test Bias

Terms, Concepts, and Names

Briefly identify the following:

Uniform Guidelines on Employee Selection Procedures_____
_____

adverse impact_____
_____

differential validity_____
_____

differential item functioning analysis (DIF)_____
_____

isodensity curve_____
_____

the case of Larry P. v. Wilson Riles_____
_____

Chitling Test_____
_____

scientific racism_____
_____

Black Intelligence Test of Cultural Homogeneity (BITCH)
_____
_____

System of Multicultural Pluralistic Assessment (SOMPA)
_____
_____

estimated learning potentials (ELP's)_____
_____

unqualified individualism_____
_____

quota system _____
_____

qualified individualism_____
_____

differential process theory_____

_____

_____

Fill-in Questions

1. Differential item functioning (DIF) analysis attempts to find test items that are _____
   _____.
2. The developers of the Black Intelliegnce Test of Cultural Homogeneity (BITCH) believed that for individuals in the black community it is more important to assess _____,
   than IQ.
3. The Black Intelligence Test of Cultural Homogeneity (BITCH) is most lacking psychometrically with regard to its _____.
4. The assumption underlying the System of Multicultural Pluralistic Assessment (SOMPA) is that cultural groups have the same _____.
5. The only component of the System of Multicultural Pluralistic Assessment (SOMPA) that is typically adopted by traditional test users and developers is the
   _____.
6. Estimated learning potentials (ELP'S) are WISC-R scores that are adjusted for _____.
7. According to the _____ approach a test is fair if it finds the best candidates for a job or for admission to school.
8. Testing experts generally agree that intelligence and aptitude tests are valid for predictive purposes, however, their major concerns involve the interpretation and application of test results by
   _____.
9. An example of the problem of finding appropriate criterion measures is seen with the Medical College Admission Test (MCAT). The MCAT predicts _____ but does not predict _____.

Multiple-Choice Questions

1. The main type of validity evidence that exists for the Chitling Test is
   a) predictive validity
   b) concurrent validity
   c) face validity
   d) content validity
   e) construct validity

2. The assessment technique which best challenges

traditional beliefs about testing is the
   a) Black Intelligence Test of Cultural Homogeneity
      (BITCH)
   b) Chitiling Test
   c) Dove Counterbalance General Intelligence Test
   d) System of Multicultural Pluaristic Assessment
      (SOMPA)
   e) none of the above

3. The System of Multicultural Pluralistic Assessment
   (SOMPA) attempts to intergrate which three approaches
   to assessment?
   a) personal, social, and organizational
   b) personal, social, and medical
   c) individual, social, and pluralistic
   d) medical, social, and pluralistic
   e) medical, communal, and intellectual

4. Which System of Multicultural Pluralistic Assessment
   (SOMPA) component uses the norms **within** a particular
   group for defining deviance?
   a) pluralistic
   b) social
   c) organizational
   d) communal
   e) medical

5. Which of the following systems takes race and sex
   differences into consideration in selection decisions?
   a) unqualified individualism
   b) qualified individualism
   c) the quota system
   d) both a and b
   e) both b and c

Thought Questions

1. Two types of validity (content and criterion) are described in relation to test bias on pages 538-545 of your text. Both approaches to defining the meaning of a test suggest that certain tests (e.g. the SAT) are in fact **not** biased or, in other words, are not differentially valid. Discuss the findings that are presented and include your reasons for agreeing or disagreeing with them.

_____

_____

_____

_____

_____

_____

_____

_____

_____

_____

_____

_____

_____

_____

_____

_____

_____

_____

_____

_____

_____

_____

2. The originator of the System of Multicultural Pluralistic Assessment (SOMPA), Jane Mercer, has argued that it is important to label as many children as posible "normal" and to remove such children from EMR classes. Her critics do not view labeling as such a damaging phenomenon and argue that these children will need special help anyway. Describe, in your opinion, what the advantages and disadvantages of the SOMPA approach are with regard to assessment and consequent placement decisions. (pgs.550-552)

_____

_____

_____

_____

_____

_____

_____

_____
_____
_____
_____
_____
_____
_____
_____
_____
_____
_____
_____
_____
_____
_____
_____
_____

3. Which model of test fairness do you prefer and why?
   (pgs.552-557)

_____
_____
_____
_____
_____
_____
_____
_____
_____
_____
_____
_____
_____
_____
_____
_____
_____
_____
_____
_____
_____
_____
_____

Answers

Terms, Concepts, and Names

Uniform Guidelines on Employee Selection Procedures (p.537)
adverse impact (p.537)
differential validity (p.538)
differential item functioning (DIF) analysis (p.540)
isodensity curve (p.542)
the case of Larry P. v. Wilson Riles (p.547)
Chitling Test (p.547)
scientific racism (p.549)
Black Intelligence Test of Cultural Homogeneity (BITCH) (p.549)
System of Multicultural Pluralistic Assessment (SOMPA) (p.550)
estimated learning potentials (ELP's) (p.552)
unqualified individualism (p.554)
quota system (p.555)
qualified individualism (p.554)
differential process theory (p.559)

Fill-in Questions

1. specifically biased against an ethnic/racial or gender group (p.540)
2. survival potential in the black community (p.549)
3. validity (p.549)
4. average potential (p.551)
5. social system component (p.551)
6. socioeconomic background (p.552)
7. unqualified individualism (p.554)
8. elementary and secondary schools (p.557)
9. success in medical school, who will be a successful doctor (p.561)

Multiple-Choice Questions

1. c (p.548)
2. d (p.550)
3. d (p.551)
4. a (p.551)
5. e (pgs.554-555)

Chapter 21

Testing and the Law

Terms, Concepts, and Names

Briefly identify the following:

interstate commerce_____
_____

control of spending_____
_____

Equal Employment Opportunity Commission (EEOC)_____
_____

four-fifths rule of adverse impact_____
_____

Truth in Testing Laws_____
_____

Education for All Handicapped Children Act of 1975_____
_____

Plessy v. Ferguson_____
_____

Brown v. Board of Education_____
_____

Stell v. Savannah-Chatham County Board of Education
_____
_____

Hobson v. Hansen_____
_____

Diana v. State Board of Education_____
_____

Larry P. v. Wilson Riles_____
_____

Parents in Action on Special Education v. Hannon_____
_____

Crawford et al. v. Honig et al._____
_____

Marchall v. Georgia _____

_____

Debra P. v. Turlington _____

_____

Regents of the University of California v. Bakke _____

_____

Golden Rule Insurance Company et al. v. Washburn et al.

_____

_____

Adarand Constructors Inc. v. Pena, Secretary of
Transportation et al. _____

_____

Griggs v. Duke Power Company _____

_____

1991 Civil Rights Act _____

_____

Connecticut v. Teal _____

_____

Americans with Disabilities Act (ADA) _____

_____

_____

Fill-in Questions

1. The major intent of the Equal Employment Opportunity
   Commission (EEOC) guidelines is to _____
   _____.

2. The New York truth in testing law was motivated by an
   investigation of _____.

3. The most controversial of the requirements set forth by
   the truth in testing law is that
   _____.

4. PL (Public Law) 94-142 guarantees a publicly financed
   education to _____.

5. The case of _____ resulted in a
   set of special provisions for the testing of
   Mexican-American and Chinese-American children.

6. The effect of the ruling of the Larry P. v. Wilson
   Riles case was that _____
   _____.

   However, the ruling of Parents in Action on Special
   Education v. Hannon concluded that_____.

7. The Bakke case was symbolic of a change in attitude about _____.
8. The 1991 Civil Rights Act clarified that the burden of proof for determining that a psychological test used in the workplace is relaible and valid is on _____.

Multiple-Choice Questions

1. One of the most interesting problems with the four-fifths rule is that
   a) most employers find it uninterpretable
   b) efforts to recruit minority group members reduce the percentage from that group that is hired
   c) typically less than four-fifths of the applicants for a given job are minorities
   d) Numerous legal loopholes in the rule result in more discrimination than took place before its adoption
   e) all of the above

2. Which of the following cases resulted in the court ruling that schools must provide nonsegregated facilities for Black and White children?
   a) Brown v. Board of Education
   b) Plessy v. Ferguson
   c) Stell v. Savannah-Chatham County Board of Education
   d) Hobson v. Hansen
   e) Diana v. State Board of Education

3. A number of cases were attempts to resist the desegragation order. Many of these cases presented test scores which suggested that Black children were genetically incapable of learning in the same classroom as white children. One such case was
   a) Hobson v. Hansen
   b) Plessy v. Ferguson
   c) Brown v. Board of Education
   d) Stell v. Savannah-Chatham County Board of Education
   e) Diana V. State Board of Education

4. The type of test that came under scrutiny in the Debra P. v. Turlington case was a
   a) standard intelligence test
   b) multicultural pluralistic test
   c) personnel test
   d) minimum competency test
   e) graduate school selection test

5. Which of the following cases resulted in the decision that employment tests must be reliable and valid?
   a) Golden Rule Insurance Company v. Washburn
   b) Griggs v. Duke Power Company
   c) Hobson v. Hansen
   d) Connecticut v. Teal
   e) Watson v. Fort Worth Bank and Trust

Thought Questions

1. The controversial third portion of the Truth in Testing Law may cause serious problems for testing programs. Several of these problems are described in your text. Discuss these issues and include your views as to whether or not this section of the law should be retained. (pgs.575-577)

_____
_____
_____
_____
_____
_____
_____
_____
_____
_____
_____
_____
_____
_____
_____
_____
_____
_____
_____
_____

2. In your opinion, what role should the courts play in the regulation of psychological tests and why?

_____
_____
_____
_____
_____
_____
_____
_____
_____

_____
_____
_____
_____
_____
_____
_____
_____
_____
_____
_____

Answers

Terms, Concepts, and Names

interstate commerce (p.567)
control of spending (p.568)
Equal Employment Opportunity Commission (EEOC) (p.568)
four-fifths rule of adverse impact (p.559)
Truth in Testing Laws (p.575)
Education for All Handicapped Children Act of 1975
(p.577)
Plessy v. Ferguson (p.578)
Brown v. Board of Education (p.578)
Stell v. Savannah-Chatham County Board of Education
(p.579)
Hobson v. Hansen (p.579)
Diana v. State Board of Education (p.580)
Larry P. v. Wilson Riles (p.581)
Parents in Action on Special Education v. Hannon
(p.584)
Crawford et al. v. Honig et al. (p.588)
Marchall v. Georgia (p.589)
Debra P. v. Turlington (p.589)
Regents of the University of California v. Bakke
(p.592)
Golden Rule Insurance Company et al. v. Washburn
et al. (p.593)
Adarand Constructors Inc. v. Pena (p.593)
Griggs v. Duke Power Company (p.595)
1991 Civil Rights Act (p.597)
Connecticut v. Teal (p.600)
Americans with Disabilites Act (ADA) (p.600)

Fill-in Questions

1. prohibit discrimination (p.569)
2. the Educational Testing Service (ETS) (p.575)
3. on request by a student, a copy of the test
   questions, correct answers, and a student's answers
   must be provided (p.576)

4. all handicapped children (p.577)
   5. Diana v. State Board of Education (p.581)
   6. IQ tests could no longer be used to place Black
      children in EMR classes (p.583); evidence of racial
      bias in standardized IQ tests was not sufficient to
      disallow their use with Black children (p.584)
   7. affirmative action programs (p.592)
   8. the employer (p.597)

Multiple-Choice Questions

   1. b (p.569)
   2. a (p.578)
   3. d (p.579)
   4. d (p.589)
   5. b (p.595)

Chapter 22

The Future of Psychological Testing

Terms, Concepts, and Names

Briefly identify the following:

theoretical concerns_____

_____

adequacy of tests_____

_____

actuarial prediction_____

_____

clinical prediction_____

_____

human rights_____

_____

labeling_____

_____

invasion of privacy_____

_____

confidentiality_____

_____

divided loyalties_____

_____

dehumanization_____

_____

usefulness of tests_____

_____

access to psychological testing services_____

_____

_____

Fill-in Questions

1. One of the most important issues underlying tests is
   the _____ of test results.

2. Most existing tests are presumed to measure a(n)_____.
3. An approach to analyzing test results which involves the use of a set of rules is called a(n)_____.
4. According to Dahlstrom (1969b), a person's privacy is only invaded when information obtained via psychological tests is used in_____.
5. In order to resolve the conflict of divided loyalties a psychologist must _____.
6. The public's general attitude toward psychological testing was described in your text as _____.
7. In the future it is likely that any test posing a real challenge to the Stanford-Binet and Wechsler tests will be based on _____ and a more comprehensive theoretical rationale.
8. In contrast to earlier predictions, the _____ is destined to be the premiere structured personality test of the twenty-first century.

Multiple-Choice Questions

1. While many individual and group tests have generally adequate reliability, just about any test could benefit from
   a) better validity documentation
   b) a larger standardization sample
   c) more representative norms
   d) simplified scoring techniques
   e) more standardized interpretations

2. Which of the following is a potential abuse inherent in the use of computer software to interpret psychological tests?
   a) use of software inappropriate to the client
   b) trivialization of assessment
   c) inadequate contribution of the clinician to the assessment process
   d) questionable computer-based interpretations
   e) all of the above

3. Current standards for test use state that the test constructor(s) must provide sufficient information to permit appropriate use of the test. Which of the following does **not** have to be included in this information?
   a) guidelines for administration and scoring
   b) information regarding item construction
   c) validity data
   d) reliability data
   e) description of the normative sample

4. The crucial social issue in testing is not whether tests are perfect but whether
   a) they are predictive of future behavior
   b) they are useful to society
   c) they can be used to make selection decisions
   d) they can measure cuurent functioning adequately
   e) they can accurately measure skills and abilities

5. Which of the following is **not** related to the increased standards of test construction?
   a) a specific published set of standards for tests
   b) improved computer technology being used in the testing field
   c) increased objectivity in test construction
   d) administration of tests to a narrower, more specific range of individuals
   e) a continuing research interest in testing

Thought Questions

1. One of the theoretical issues underlying the use of psychological tests involves the stability of human characteristics. Using the information presented on pages 606-609 of your text as a framework discuss your views on this topic.

_____
_____
_____
_____
_____
_____
_____
_____
_____
_____
_____
_____
_____
_____
_____
_____
_____
_____
_____
_____
_____
_____
_____

2. Discuss some of the negative consequences of "labeling" as presented on page 611-612 of your text. What might be some positive aspects of labeling? Discuss these as well.

_____
_____
_____
_____
_____
_____
_____
_____
_____
_____
_____
_____
_____
_____
_____
_____
_____
_____
_____
_____

Answers

Terms, Concepts, and Names

theoretical concerns (p.606)
adequacy of tests (p.609)
actuarial prediction (p.610)
clinical prediction (p.610)
human rights (p.611)
labeling (p.611)
invasion of privacy (p.612)
confidentiality (p.612)
divided loyalties (p.613)
dehumanization (p.615)
usefulness of tests (p.615)
access to psychological testing services (p.616)

Fill-in Questions

1. dependability (reliability) (p.606)
2. stable entity (p.607)
3. actuarial approach (p.610)
4. inappropriate ways (p.612)

5. inform all concerned as to where his/her loyalty
   lies (p.613)
6. ambivalent (p.620)
7. original concepts (p.623)
8. MMPI-2 (p.623)

Multiple-Choice Questions

1. a (p.610)
2. e (p.610)
3. b (p.614)
4. b (p.616)
5. d (pgs.618-620)